# Love More, Sin Less

---

*Developing a God-Shaped Heart*

---

# Love More, Sin Less

---

*Developing a God-Shaped Heart*

---

*Aubrey Johnson*

Gospel Advocate Company
Nashville, Tennessee

## Other Books by Aubrey Johnson

*The Barnabas Factor: Realize Your Encouragement Potential*

*Renewing Your Spiritual Life: Thirteen Simple Steps for Maximum Spiritual Growth*

*Spiritual Patriots: Jude's Call to Arms*

Published by Gospel Advocate Co.
1006 Elm Hill Pike, Nashville, TN 37210
http://www.gospeladvocate.com

ISBN-10: 0-89225-563-3
ISBN-13: 978-0-89225-563-4

*God is love, and he who abides in love abides in God,*
*and God in him.* –1 John 4:16

## *Dedication*

To my wife Lisa, without whose insistence and inspiration this book would not have been written; my sister Paula, for our conversations that first clarified my thinking on this subject; and all who are passionately seeking God in the 21st century. May this new lens help you see the enduring beauty of the ancient gospel.

## *Acknowledgments*

I would like to thank my professors from the Doctor of Ministry Program at Gordon-Conwell Theological Seminary (Charlotte campus) for challenging my thinking on the role of love as it relates to the mission of Christ's church and Christian leadership:

Dr. Wayne Goodwin
Dr. Steve Klipowicz
Dr. Tim Laniak
Dr. Jack Lindburg
Dr. Bill Mayer
Dr. Bill Murray

I am also grateful for the contributions of six very special friends:

Kyle Butt
Houston Bynum
Dr. Earl Edwards
Lonnie Jones
Ron Stough
Greg Tidwell

# Table of Contents

# Foreword

Wow! Rarely do I read things that are said in a way in which I wish I had said them. This new work is truly inspiring. It reminds, reveals, rebukes and revitalizes.

The most damaging cancer to invade any relationship is selfishness. In fact, selfishness is the common denominator to all sin (James 1:13; 3:16). The opposite of selfishness is love. Often we have focused our energies on avoiding sinful activities. Yet if we refocus on hitting the target of love, we then fulfill all the requirements for relationships with God and people. "Love does no harm to a neighbor; therefore love is the fulfillment of the law" (Romans 13:10). So then instead of living to avoid sin and being controlled by a reactive lifestyle our goal is to pursue love. Thus the Christian lifestyle is not merely to sin less, but rather to love more. If sin is "missing the mark," then Aubrey has clearly defined the mark that we cannot miss.

Lonnie Jones, M.S., L.P.C., N.C.C.

# The Majesty
# of Love

God's purpose for your life is found in the New Testament. Like two great pillars, the Great Commission and the Great Commandment provide the supporting structure for the teaching in each New Testament book. Yet even these pillars are not equal; one is the true weight-bearing axis of Christianity. When a person perceives the red-hot center of God's will, it enlightens the mind, stirs the heart, and activates the will as nothing else can. The clearer a person becomes about this overarching purpose, the more confident and effective he becomes as a spiritual being. Therefore, it is vital to grasp the hub around which everything revolves in the Christian faith – a heart and life of love!

Once this unifying purpose is discovered, it provides the key for understanding the Christian life as a whole. Love, therefore, is the spark underlying the entire process of Christian faith and growth. To live effectively and confidently, Christians must grasp not only the primacy of love but also how it interrelates with other biblical ideas. In other words, it is impossible to understand the nature of sin, the significance of faith, the danger of unbelief, the meaning of salvation, the goal of sanctification, the power of fellowship, or the joy of service without taking into account how love weighs on each of these concepts. The aim of this book is to help you examine the connection between love and other foundational components of Christianity and, thereby, to unleash the gospel's power to produce an astounding and enduring change in your life. By loving more, you will sin less. It is that simple.

# About This Book

The 13 chapters of this book fall under six section headings: the loving call, mind, choice, path, church and God. The idea was to take a close look at the various parts of God's plan of redemption and ask, "What's love got to do with it?" The answer came back loud and clear: "Everything!" Jesus' love redeems human hearts and restores health to relationships. His followers are loving people characterized by spiritual integrity, amazing self-awareness, high levels of accountability, continuous growth, caring associations, and intimacy with God. Above all else, Christianity is a religion of love.

*Section 1, The Loving Call – Love is about seeking renewal.*
- The gospel is heaven's invitation to a life of love.
- Sin is Satan's summons to a life of selfishness.

*Section 2, The Loving Mind – Love is about facing reality.*
- Faith brings clarity about the nature of love.
- Unbelief creates confusion about the meaning of love.

*Section 3, The Loving Choice – Love is about taking responsibility.*
- Repentance directs searching hearts to a more loving future.
- Salvation delivers sorrowful hearts from an unloving past.

*Section 4, The Loving Path – Love is about increasing righteousness.*
- Sanctification accelerates growth in love.
- Temptation assesses growth in love.

*Section 5, The Loving Church – Love is about improving relationships.*
- Fellowship is sharing one another's greatest blessings.
- Restoration is bearing one another's heaviest burdens.
- Evangelism is meeting one another's deepest needs.

*Section 6, The Loving God – Love is about reflecting God's radiance.*
- Hope is the confidence that comes from trusting God's love.
- Unity is the closeness that comes from emulating God's love.

At the end of each chapter, you will find study questions (answers on page 157) and a survey to assist you in your quest for a more loving life. The key to building a great life (and a great church) is a great commitment to the Great Commandment. May God bless you as you read on and discover the full extent of love's power to enrich your life.

# The Loving Call

*"But above all these things put on love,
which is the bond of perfection." – Colossians 3:14*

The call of the gospel is a call to love. We are summoned by God's love to share in the fellowship of loving spirits in heaven and on earth (Philippians 2:1-2). Making a commitment to a love-based life is the best decision one can ever make: the world makes sense as never before, decisions are brought into sharper focus, and life is more satisfying, although no less challenging. In the first chapter of this book, the call to love is shown to be the primary duty of mankind. It is the purpose for which we were created and the basis by which we shall be judged. In the second chapter, a careful examination will be made of sin and its power to undermine our intention to love. Two forces are at work in every human heart: the urge to love and the urge to sin. Which will you choose?

Chapter 1

# *Love Exalted:* Gospel

*"Ultimately love is everything." – M. Scott Peck*

I f I could choose one word to summarize the teachings of the Bible, it would be "relationship." Some would argue for other words such as "sin" or "salvation," but what are the meanings of those terms apart from association with others? Sin has to do with severing wholesome relationships, and salvation has to do with restoring right relationships that have been damaged by sin. Remove the interpersonal element and Christianity is more than diminished; it loses its very meaning.

Still, one may be skeptical about the possibility of making "relationships" the overarching theme of the Bible. It sounds as if a plea is being made to minimize the authority of Scripture and replace it with pure subjectivism. Nothing could be further from the truth. The fact is that those who are most committed to honoring the full intent of the Bible's teaching enjoy the healthiest possible ties. Only sound doctrine can produce sound relationships. The primacy of relationships is not an artificial grid imposed upon Scripture, it is the inevitable conclusion of a careful reading of God's Word. That is why the most important teaching of the Christian faith is the centrality of love.

The gospel is good news precisely because it is a message of love. It tells of gracious love for ungodly sinners (Romans 5:6-8) and patient love for unruly saints (1 Thessalonians 5:14-15). In its essence, it is a call to embrace and emulate the love of God (Matthew 28:18-20). Those who accept this calling cast aside selfishness and commit themselves to a lifetime of growth in love. Improved relationships marked by increasing intimacy are the end result of building one another up in love.

## The First Commandment

Every religious and ethical ordinance in the Bible is designed to promote a loving relationship with the Father and those created in His image. Scripture is explicit and repetitive in assigning love as the highest priority of Jesus' disciples. One day the Lord was approached by a scribe who asked, "Which is the first commandment of all?"

> Jesus answered him, "The first of all the commandments is: 'Hear, O Israel, the Lord our God, the Lord is one. And you shall love the Lord your God with all your heart, with all your soul, with all your mind, and with all your strength.' This is the first commandment. And the second, like it, is this: 'You shall love your neighbor as yourself.' There is no other commandment greater than these" (Mark 12:29-31).

By referencing Moses (Deuteronomy 6:4-5; Leviticus 19:18), Jesus demonstrated that love had been the guiding principle of God's people from the very beginning. After delivering the Great Commandment, He added these remarkable words: "On these two commandments hang all the law and the prophets" (Matthew 22:40). Paul made a similar pronouncement when he declared that the whole law is fulfilled in the word "love" (Galatians 5:14). James referred to this treasured teaching as "the royal law" (James 2:8). Indeed, it is the ruling principle from which all other biblical instruction is derived.

The challenge of the Christian life is to spur one another to love and engage in good works (Hebrews 10:24). A loving disposition is not enough; inner attitudes must be confirmed by outward expressions of love (Galatians 5:6). The church is to be God's example of the possibility and beauty of loving relationships. For this reason the Hebrews writer exhorted, "Let brotherly love continue" (Hebrews 13:1).

# *John's Teaching on Love*

The primacy of love was not an isolated teaching of our Lord; it was and remains the heart of the gospel. That is why Jesus heralded brotherly love as the distinguishing mark of genuine discipleship: "By this all will know that you are My disciples, if you have love for one another" (John 13:35). This is the language of mission. Love is the leading sign of Christlikeness and the focal point of the faith once delivered to the saints. But what does it mean to love like Jesus?

• *The Conduct of Love.* The apostle John was most helpful in clearing up misunderstandings about love. John explained that biblical love involves behavior and not merely sentiment: "This is love, that we walk according to His commandments" (2 John 6). Love involves performance (walk) and not just profession (talk). Every precept of Christ advances this holy purpose, yet one command excels all others.

Jesus announced, "This is my commandment, that you love one another as I have loved you" (John 15:12). It is a mistake to conclude from this broad pronouncement that Christ's concern was limited to His followers' feelings. The Lord was not minimizing the specifics of Scripture in favor of a vague emotional experience; He was highlighting the purpose behind all His instructions (14:15). In fact, acts of righteousness are nothing more than loving acts (1 John 3:10). Every instance of heartfelt obedience is an expression of tender affection for the Father. Those who claim to love God while disregarding His revealed will merely delude themselves. Likewise, those who claim to love God while ignoring the needs and consciences of their fellowman are equally self-deceived (1 John 4:7-8, 12, 20-21).

• *The Goal of Love.* Love in a Christian context must be distinguished from its popular usage in society. Nowhere in Scripture is that difference made plainer than in John 3:16: "For God so loved the world that He gave His only begotten Son, that whoever believes in Him should not perish but have everlasting life."

According to John, divine love is …

• More active than passive.
• More generous than grasping.
• More redemptive than coddling.

Therefore, love is a conscious choice rather than an unpredictable sentiment. A Christian who understands love biblically is devoted to serving others in ways that promote their development as human beings. As ministers of reconciliation, they assist others in overcoming hindrances to transformation and unity (2 Corinthians 5:17-21). The goal of love is to allow growth in Christlikeness and community.

Love stretches the soul to fulfill the potential placed within it at creation. It moves one closer to the image of oneness shared by members of the Godhead. Love is the opposite of sin and the answer to its disruptive effects in relationships. It is the antidote to alienation from divinity, humanity and one's true identity.

• *The Scope of Love.* In Jesus' final prayer before going to Gethsemane, He interceded on behalf of His disciples with these words: "And I have declared to them Your name, and will declare it, that the love with which You loved Me may be in them, and I in them" (John 17:26). Love is the most defining characteristic of God (1 John 4:7-8), and those who truly know God and are born of God aspire to love as He loves. Therefore, the love that Jesus approves must extend to all people and not just those with pleasing personalities (John 3:16):

• Love is for the sinful and stubborn as well as the sweet.
• It is a deliberate decision rather than a fleeting feeling.
• It is a continuing commitment rather than a momentary mood.
• Love is refined intention rather than raw emotion.

## Paul's Teaching on Love

Paul emphasized the centrality of love throughout his ministry. He saw the obligation to love as a welcome but neverending debt (Romans 13:8). In cataloguing the evidence of the Spirit in a believer's life, love topped his list (Galatians 5:22). He placed it above all other Christian virtues, suggesting that they are merely facets of the more fundamental quality of love (Colossians 3:14).

• *The Breadth of Love.* Paul taught that those who love their neighbor automatically fulfill Moses' law. Because the design of the Ten Commandments was to discourage self-centered behavior that damages relationships, Paul drew the following conclusion: "Love does no harm to a neighbor; therefore love is the fulfillment of the law" (Romans 13:10).

Love is simply relating to others responsibly. It is striving to meet the needs of fellow human beings in ways that do not compromise their character or interfere with their personal development. Genuine love is valuing people, attending to their needs, and supporting their growth. Love occurs when higher interests prevail over selfish interests.

I love others when I deny myself to contribute to their betterment. I love myself when I let go of harmful attitudes and habits to become an improved version of myself. Love maximizes the spiritual potential of both lover and beloved. The ultimate aim is to become more like Christ (Galatians 2:20).

Paul came to see that every divine directive is a call to love. After citing four of the Ten Commandments, he commented, "[A]nd if there is any other commandment, are all summed up in the saying, namely, 'You shall love your neighbor as yourself' " (Romans 13:9). Love is the mission of Jesus' church because every biblical mandate clarifies how love should be manifested in a particular context. Even the Great Commission is subservient to the Great Commandment because evangelism was commanded by Christ as love's response to a lost soul's need.

Eight of the nine virtues Paul listed as fruit of the Spirit are really just demonstrations of love at work. For example, to be joyful (Philippians 4:4), pursue peace (Hebrews 12:14), and suffer long (Ephesians 4:2) are all New Testament commands. If every command is summed up in the charge to love, then each of these terms is nothing more than a description of the way love adapts itself to the need or circumstance at hand.

• *The Depth of Love.* Nowhere is Paul's view of love more evident than in his ministry to the church in Corinth. He dealt with the intercongregational difficulties of the Corinthians by undertaking a two-fold strategy. First, he addressed a few of the specific problems undermining their peace and fellowship. Then, he went to the root of the problem underlying all of their difficulties – a lack of love (1 Corinthians 13:1-13).

Rather than trying to sort out all the minutiae of their interpersonal conflicts, the apostle began lifting them above their petty disputes. If they loved each other more, most of their disagreements would fade away. It is impossible to make enough rules to deal with every problem that can arise. At some point, people must be directed to a more comprehensive solution that will help them transcend their troubles.

Paul argued that no spiritual achievement could substitute for a deficiency in love (1 Corinthians 13:1-3). The most powerful words one could speak, the most insightful thoughts one could think and the most stirring sacrifice one could make would be worthless unless grounded in genuine concern for others. All of a person's abilities, gifts and possessions are trusts for blessing our fellowman. No matter how astounding a person's accomplishments, a life that revolves around self is absolutely meaningless.

• *The Height of Love.* After magnificently describing love in action (1 Corinthians 13:4-7), Paul concluded by exalting the greatness of love (v. 13). Faith, hope and love are frequently mentioned as the surpassing qualities of Christian character (Romans 5:1-5; Galatians 5:5; Ephesians 4:2-5; 1 Thessalonians 1:3; 5:8). However, as great as faith and hope are, love excels them in two critical ways. First, faith and hope are temporary provisions, whereas love is both eternal and invincible. Second, faith and hope are a means to an end, whereas love is the end itself.

This vital distinction between means and end is illustrated by Paul's teaching on the role of knowledge in a Christian's life. The apostle explained that "Knowledge puffs up, but love edifies" (1 Corinthians 8:1). Was Paul belittling the value of knowledge? By no means! In fact, he urged his readers to grow in love by increasing knowledge (Philippians 1:9). Love must be informed, but knowledge is a tool rather than the goal, which is to love more and better. Therefore, Paul summarized his message with these concluding words: "Let all that you do be done with love" (1 Corinthians 16:14).

## Life's Highest Value

From this brief survey of Scripture, it is evident that love is not one virtue among many in the Christian faith, but the supreme virtue from which all others derive their essence. Therefore, to practice and promote love is the mission of Christ's church. Understanding this fact does not diminish the particulars of God's precepts; it simply explains precisely why each command should be faithfully observed. Each one sheds light on how love is best expressed in a particular context and reveals how love is best sustained within a community of believers.

It is easy to see how the ethical instructions of the Bible protect loving relationships. Most people understand how human ties are harmed by immoral behaviors such as dishonesty and drunkenness; yet love is the basis of the religious instructions of the Bible as well. Through direct commands and inspired precedents, the Lord has provided the spiritual infrastructure to sustain the church as a loving community. Those who ignore or attempt to improve upon what God has provided make two serious mistakes. First, any deviation from the apostles' doctrine cannot produce an equal effect. In other words, God's way is best suited to accomplish His purpose. Second, departures from the biblical standard easily become points of disagreement and division. Therefore, accurate interpretation of Scripture and faithful observance of biblical teaching are indications of love rather than legalism.

## *Avoiding Extremes*

Yet it is possible to become mired in the finer details of God's commands and miss the main point. Who has not encountered someone stressing adherence to outward forms of Christianity but displaying a hateful attitude toward those who failed to appreciate the value of those commandments? Or who has not witnessed congregational turf wars in which members engaging in good works feuded over resources or interpretations of the congregation's policies and procedures? These examples demonstrate why it is vital to restore love to its preeminent place in Christian thought and practice.

Unfortunately, the priority of love is sometimes used as a pretext for sacrificing commitment to inspired patterns and particulars of Scripture that give Christ's church its unique identity. Evidence of this confusion can be seen in preachers who proclaim values but not judgment, elders who exalt Christ but diminish His church, teachers who instruct on forgiveness but not repentance, youth workers who entertain but do not edify, ministries that fill stomachs but not souls, and missions that heal bodies but not spirits. Holding religious services, rendering humanitarian aid, and sustaining a pious bureaucracy are not the same as fulfilling the church's charge to eradicate sin through proclaiming the good news of Christ's love. However, a tendency also exists to stress the specifics of Scripture without seeing how they are related to the larger theme of love.

Therefore, clarity regarding the church's mission can help Christians avoid both of these extremes and their detrimental effects.

James declared, "Where do wars and fights come from among you? Do they not come from your desires for pleasure that war in your members?" (James 4:1). Church fusses, like all forms of conflict, are the direct result of a failure to love sufficiently. They come from the desire to have things my way rather than considering the needs of others and the well-being of the church as a whole. It is shocking that bitterness of this kind frequently occurs among brethren whose ministry objectives get at cross-purposes. James' solution for the worldliness that plagued the church was for combatants to purify their hearts (James 4:8). If opponents focused on the church's ultimate mission rather than immediate goals, peace would prevail.

## Warmed by Love

Christ and His apostles were aware of multiple objectives underlying their ministries, but over them all was a central unifying purpose that informed and energized the others. These lofty yet lesser aims are like squares of fabric sewn together to make one large, warm quilt. Like one who wrestles with short covers on a wintry night, those who attempt to find comfort in any single part will find it insufficient for their needs. One reason for confusion and discouragement among Christians is that they do not grasp the whole of God's mission for the church. Instead, they cling to smaller pieces of purpose rather than the composite quilt that covers all that Christians are to become and do. The common thread running throughout Christ's teaching is the centrality of love (Matthew 22:37-39). So pull up the covers, turn the page and start warming your soul!

## Questions

1. What single word summarizes the teachings of the Bible?

2. What is the most important teaching of the Christian faith?

3. Sin and salvation cannot be understood apart from what?

4. What is the biblical term for what severs wholesome relationships?

5. What is the biblical term for restoring right relationships damaged by sin?

6. What percentage of the Bible's commandments is designed to promote loving relationships with God and fellowman?

7. What can people discern from the way Christians love one another?

8. If knowledge puffs up, what does love do?

9. What did James say is the result of desiring to have things my way rather than considering the needs of others and the welfare of the church?

10. What is the supreme virtue from which all others derive their essence?

## *Discussion Questions*

1. How does understanding love as the mission of the church change your view of Christianity?

2. Does the idea of "relationships" as the overarching theme of the Bible make you feel excited or uneasy?

3. How does pursuing secondary goals without reference to the primary goal create problems?

4. How are you hoping to benefit from this study?

5. Memorize "The Lover's Prayer" on the next page and use it over the next 13 weeks as you begin each day. It will help you to recall what you have studied and remind you to put it into practice. Each line of the prayer comes from the section headings in the table of contents.

6. Complete the Love Quest Survey each week to assess your progress in developing a more loving life. Your efforts will be rewarded by increased spiritual health and improved relationships.

# The Lover's Prayer

Dear God,
Help me to …

Accept the loving call,
Adopt the loving mind,
Make the loving choice,
Complete the loving climb,
Embrace the loving church,
And love Your Son divine.

# Love Quest Survey
## Pursuing a God-Shaped Heart

### Love More      (Rate your progress this week)

My love skills (behaviors that make me MORE loving)    Better – Worse

1. Honesty (realistic, truthful, self-aware)    ❏    ❏
2. Empathy (thoughtful, compassionate, kind, forgiving)    ❏    ❏
3. Responsibility (accountable, reliable, disciplined)    ❏    ❏

My love opportunities – Mark 12:30-31

• God (loving enthusiastically – without reservation)    Better – Worse

1. With all my heart (warm, affectionate love)    ❏    ❏
2. With all my mind (intelligent, informed love)    ❏    ❏
3. With all my strength (energetic, devoted love)    ❏    ❏
4. With all my soul (integrated, holistic love)    ❏    ❏

• Others (loving empathetically – doing good, not harm)    Better – Worse

| | | | | | Better – Worse |
|---|---|---|---|---|---|
| 1. My mate | ❏ | ❏ | 5. My child | ❏ | ❏ |
| 2. My best friend | ❏ | ❏ | 6. My boss | ❏ | ❏ |
| 3. My co-worker | ❏ | ❏ | 7. My neighbor | ❏ | ❏ |
| 4. My enemy | ❏ | ❏ | 8. My encounters with strangers | ❏ | ❏ |

• Self (loving effectively – bringing out my best self)    Better – Worse

1. My body (caring for my physical needs and health)    ❏    ❏
2. My heart (caring for my emotional needs and self-esteem) ❏    ❏
3. My mind (caring for my intellectual needs and growth)    ❏    ❏
4. My soul (caring for my spiritual needs and destiny)    ❏    ❏

### Sin Less      (Rate your progress this week)

• My sin snares (behaviors that make me LESS loving)    Better – Worse

1. Irrationality (unrealistic, unaware, untruthful)    ❏    ❏
2. Fabricating (exaggerating, demonizing, romanticizing)    ❏    ❏
3. Insensitivity (uncaring, unkind, unmindful)    ❏    ❏
4. Irresponsibility (undisciplined, unreliable, unaccountable) ❏    ❏

• My sin challenges (ways I hurt the people I profess to love) Better – Worse

1. Tongue (gossiping, criticizing, blaming, lying)    ❏    ❏
2. Temper (anger, negativity, intimidation)    ❏    ❏
3. Temptations (lust, pride, selfishness, laziness)    ❏    ❏

## My Loving Journal (developing my love-consciousness)

• I felt loved last week when …
• Loving choices I made last week:
• Unloving choices I made last week:
• This week I will love more by …
• This week I will sin less by …

# Chapter 2

# *Love Subverted:* Sin

*"Sin is broken relationship, the distortion of the image of God in us. Sin, in other words, disorders and fractures our capacity for communion." – Catherine Mowry LaCugna*

I f the Bible were a museum, it would house two great exhibits on the origin of sin. One would display the colossal error of angels whose pride and discontent led to an ill-fated uprising in heaven. The other would highlight the first human sin, when ungrateful mortals betrayed their Creator in hopes of becoming like Him. The costliness of sin is startling when looking at these examples. The angels gave up their place in heaven; Adam and Eve forfeited their home in Eden. No less is at stake in our own struggle with sin. But why would anyone risk so much? How can such a gamble be explained?

Sin continues to dominate most people's lives today. Although all humans are sinners (Romans 3:23; 1 John 1:8), the Bible maintains that life does not have to be sin-controlled (Romans 6:14). Through faith in Christ, imperfect people can rise above sinful urges and enjoy holier lives and healthier relationships.

With this in mind, let us undertake a careful investigation of this thing called "sin." We will seek to comprehend the underlying dynamics that make it such a powerful force. We will also calculate its immense costs and comprehend the terrible consequences experienced by those who yield themselves to it. Through our study, our appreciation for love will increase and our attraction to sin will decrease.

## What Is Sin?

We will begin by constructing a working definition of sin that clearly communicates both its ugliness and costliness. A variety of Hebrew and Greek words were used to represent this concept in Scripture, and each one tells more of the story of sin's hurtfulness.

• *Missing the Mark.* One Bible word, *hamartia*, depicts sin as "missing the mark" (Matthew 1:21; Romans 6:23). Like an arrow that strays from its target, human intentions often fall short of their supreme objective. But what is the mark? The chief aim of every Christian is a life of love; therefore, love is the mark. Some will dissent, "No, the mark is the word of God," but what is the central message of the Bible if not love? Others will argue that the goal is conforming to God's nature, but what would it mean to be like God if not to love?

• *Trespass.* Another Bible term for sin means "to side-step" (Matthew 6:14; Galatians 6:1; Ephesians 2:1, 5). This word for infringing on someone's property line came to stand for breaching God's will. But what is the line that has been inappropriately crossed? The answer can be found in Paul's description of love as a "more excellent way" (1 Corinthians 12:31). Christians are continually exhorted to walk in the pathway of love (2 John 4-6). When saints commit a sin, they violate healthy relational boundaries.

• *Lawlessness.* Sin is sometimes described as "lawbreaking." John wrote, "Whoever commits sin also commits lawlessness, and sin is lawlessness" (1 John 3:4). But what law has been violated? According to Paul, every sin, regardless of its specific nature, infringes on the law of love (Galatians 5:14).

## What Does Sin Do?

No matter which Bible word one chooses to convey the idea of sin, it must essentially be understood as a violation of the Great Commandment. Sin is an affront to love because every biblical teaching was designed to strengthen relationships. Therefore, when any of God's ethical or religious instructions is disregarded, the offender's relationships will be damaged in some way. Sin must also be understood as relational because whenever a person sins, he sins against someone. Whether that sin is against a family member (Luke 15:18-21), a brother in Christ (Matthew 18:15), an authority figure (1 Peter 2:13-17), or oneself (1 Corinthians 6:18), it is ultimately an offense against God. When resisting the advances of Potiphar's wife, Joseph pleaded, "How then can I do this great wickedness, and sin against God" (Genesis 39:9). When it comes to sin, injured party number one is always the Lord. David's adultery with Bathsheba led to this poetic confession of wrongdoing: "Against You, You only, have I sinned, and done this evil in Your sight" (Psalm 51:4). David believed that the one hurt first and most by sin was the Lord. That is because sin not only disregards the law but the Lawgiver. It is not only a challenge to His sovereignty, it is a denial of His worthiness to receive love, worship and obedience.

Athanasius said that the glory of God is the perfection of the creature. Love perfects humanity (Colossians 3:14). Sin, on the other hand, degrades and divides mankind (Romans 3:23). Therefore, when love expands and peace abounds, the Lord is glorified. When love contracts and discord prevails, He is grieved.

So once again, "What is sin?"

• It is an unloving behavior or attitude (Matthew 5:27-28).
• Sin can be a single concrete act or a ruling principle that overshadows the entirety of one's thoughts and life (Ephesians 2:1-3).
• It can be a passive lack of concern for others (Genesis 4:9) or an active attempt to injure someone (v. 8).

That is why God hates sin, and every Christian should too. Sin damages relationships! But if it is so harmful, what is the attraction? Why do people keep sinning? Why do they make messes and deny any responsibility for what they create? And why do people repeat patterns of behavior that produce disappointing and sinful results? To answer these questions, it is necessary to explore the dynamics of sin.

## How Does Sin Work?

• *The Adversary.* When addressing the subject of spiritual warfare, Paul exhorted Christians to "stand against the wiles of the devil" (Ephesians 6:11). The word "wiles" refers to a well thought-out strategy. Satan's enticements are not like random drive-by shootings. His servants follow a carefully devised plan that has proven its effectiveness over thousands of years.

Satan's tactics begin with psychological warfare because sin is more likely to occur when the mind is underutilized. The brain is a tool for thinking, and disordered thinking lies at the root of disobedience. Delusion and defiance result from mishandling one's mental capacities. That is why Satan specializes in confusing the mind and quieting the conscience (2 Corinthians 11:3).

• *The Accomplice.* The devil is unequaled in the art of spiritual seduction, but he cannot succeed without the cooperation of his quarry. Guarding the heart and protecting the mind are sacred duties that cannot be delegated. The responsibility for mind management rests with each individual. Peter admonished, "Therefore gird up the loins of your mind, be sober, and rest your hope fully upon the grace that is to be brought to you at the revelation of Jesus Christ; as obedient children, not conforming yourselves to the former lusts, as in your ignorance" (1 Peter 1:13-14). The key to a wiser life is accepting responsibility for thoughts and their consequences.

• *The Advice.* Knowing mankind's accountability and Satan's trickery, Paul cautioned believers to, "[t]est all things; hold fast what is good" (1 Thessalonians 5:21). But how are ideas, beliefs and values tested for goodness? Here are four suggestions:

(1) Check with scripture (Acts 17:11). Are my beliefs biblical (2 Timothy 2:15)?

(2) Check with counselors (Proverbs 11:14). Are they blameless (Philippians 4:8)?

(3) Check their fruits (Matthew 7:15-20). Are they beneficial (James 3:17)?

(4) Check your heart (Matthew 7:12). Are my beliefs benevolent (Romans 13:10)?

Most sins stem from the inability to empathize with other human beings (Matthew 7:12). One may view his behavior as helpful or even heroic when it is actually harmful and self-serving. Sinful deeds and desires can be rationalized in multiple ways:

(1) Devaluing the person sinned against.

(2) Denying the destructive nature of my actions.

(3) Downplaying the extent of another's suffering.

(4) Deciding someone deserves what he gets.

(5) Disregarding the selfishness of my motives.

When a person disables his conscience and disengages from reality, he loses his primary defense system. At that point, he becomes easy prey for the enemy. The goal of immobilizing the conscience is to evade honest evaluation of thoughts and actions while lessening internal conflict or guilt. Some use addictive chemicals to do the job. Others develop an uncanny capacity to shut down the conscience at will. In a kind of Jekyll and Hyde experience, they silence the good urges that appeal to their better instincts while heightening the passions that excite the flesh.

When the mind's higher (spiritual and intellectual) capacities are rendered inoperative, the brain is still functional on a non-critical or brute level. Words and images are used to produce powerful thoughts and emotions that stimulate sensual desire. Through the use of association, Satan undertakes systematic neurological training to link sensations of pleasure with sights, sounds and smells. The colorful bottles on the shelves of a pub have a magical allure to an alcoholic and the scent of an illicit lover's perfume can instantly ignite passion. A mere word can trigger subconscious memories that create intense reactions known in biblical terminology as "lust." The ability to associate pleasurable experiences with past sin strengthens their hold upon the heart.

The body is the organic instrument of indwelling sin (Romans 6:6). Through repeated exposure, the neurological sensations derived from the anticipation of wrongdoing become nearly irresistible. With each new episode, sin digs in deeper and fortifies its mental and physiological strongholds (Ephesians 4:27).

## Solutions to Sin

• *Christ.* When attempts are made to break this self-reinforcing cycle of sin, the loss of pleasure can seem almost unbearable. Those who try to grit their teeth and bear up under the strain can achieve marginal success in the short term, but they cannot maintain the level of consciousness and commitment necessary to succeed in the long run. The only lasting solution is to transform the mind and heart. Willpower alone is insufficient to sustain the fight against sin. To defeat sin one must stop loving it.

The solution to sin is love for Christ, and that love is initially displayed in one's conversion to Christ. The next four chapters will explain the conversion process and what occurs both spiritually and psychologically. Yet one who loves Christ can still struggle with conduct that is unbecoming to a believer. In chapters 7 through 13, we will look at God's plan for maturing Christians and enabling them to overcome residual and habitual sin. In the meantime, a few words regarding honesty and integrity will help to frame the discussion that will follow.

*• Integrity.* Sin is a symptom of a divided heart. When love for God is fully integrated, sin has no foothold from which to launch an attack (Mark 12:30). Yet love for sin can linger in places hidden from the conscious mind (James 1:21). Its presence is betrayed by its fruit. Acts of spiritual sabotage reveal a sinister force at work, undermining good intentions (Romans 7:15-23) and indicating a splintered soul.

Constant clashes between values and desires drain the spirit of its strength. Integrity is the alignment of thoughts, feelings and actions. It is knowing God's will and gladly doing it (1 John 5:3; 2 Corinthians 9:7). When beliefs and behavior do not correspond, the conflict produces spiritual weakness or sickness. Healing requires divine grace and a deepening of faith to correct the blockage created by selfishness.

Sin is an obstruction of the Spirit that occurs when the flow of love is restricted in some portion of a person's life. The church is the critical response team that works to restore wholeness to sin-damaged hearts. Healthy love is not possible apart from closer ties with God's Word and His people. Faith and fellowship are good medicine for the soul.

*• Honesty.* To stop loving sin, one must think differently about sin. It must be disassociated from the former good feelings it aroused. In a kind of "Spiritual Reality Therapy," Christians must be able to show others the destructive, life-depleting consequences of sinful behavior (Proverbs 7:22-23). When seen in its true light, sin loses its appeal. When associated with exposure, shame, scandal, incarceration or disease, what was once alluring becomes repulsive and undesirable. Without exception, sinful longings have their basis in illusion.

Preaching and teaching are God's means of breaking the hold of sin and retraining the mind to react differently to the old stimuli. The gospel corrects delusional thinking and its erroneous associations. Only hearts devoted to God and truth can experience abundant life and responsible relationships.

## Life's Basic Question

Righteous living is a result of loving the right things. That is why Solomon counseled, "Keep your heart with all diligence, for out of it spring the issues of life" (Proverbs 4:23). Conversely, sinful living is the result of loving the wrong things. John wrote, "Do not love the world or the things in the world. If anyone loves the world, the love of the Father is not in him" (1 John 2:15). Similarly, Paul taught, "Set your mind on things above, not on things on the earth" (Colossians 3:2).

Sin is the chief symptom of a spiritual attachment disorder, albeit one that is freely chosen. Those who place love of possessions (materialism) and pleasure (hedonism) above loving God and man will experience untold misery due to misplaced priorities (1 Timothy 6:9-10). Obsessive behaviors are products of irrational desires that have taken possession of the mind. Therefore, the most fundamental question of life is, "What or whom do I love?"

## Decision Time

The mind is the field upon which life's battles are fought, and each individual must decide the victor. Will love or sin prevail? When the moment of decision comes, those who think clearly and honestly are in the best position to choose responsibly from life's options.

Popular thought seldom contains the most constructive and helpful answers to relational difficulties. By thinking biblically, it is possible to escape the contaminated current of culture. When streams of thought are polluted by selfishness, they produce mental distortions, making it difficult to distinguish truth from falsehood. Like conservationists committed to reclaiming tainted water supplies, Christians must passionately commit themselves to being clearheaded and pure in thought.

Because sin is rooted in mental distortions of the way life and relationships work, Scripture is a Christian's touchstone with reality and fellowship with the heavenly Father (1 John 1:7). It is also the supreme guide for loving, life-enhancing relationships with others. Those who believe the Word of God and order their lives by its teaching partake in the solution to sin and its alienating properties. In the next chapter, we will take a closer look at how faith corrects faulty thinking and selfish living.

## Questions

1. Who committed the first sin?

2. Who committed the second sin?

3. What is the meaning of "sin"?

4. What mark has been missed, line transgressed or law broken?

5. Sin is an affront to love because it damages what?

6. Whenever a person sins, he sins against what?

7. Who is sin against first and foremost?

8. Sin works best when what does not function properly?

9. In what kind of warfare does Satan engage?

10. What is a Christian's touchstone with reality and fellowship with God?

## Discussion Questions

1. Why does willpower alone fail in overcoming habitual sin?

2. Why is the basic question of life, "What or whom do you love?"

3. Describe how sin operates.

# Love Quest Survey
## Pursuing a God-Shaped Heart

### Love More           (Rate your progress this week)

My love skills (behaviors that make me MORE loving)    Better – Worse
1. Honesty (realistic, truthful, self-aware)    ❏    ❏
2. Empathy (thoughtful, compassionate, kind, forgiving)    ❏    ❏
3. Responsibility (accountable, reliable, disciplined)    ❏    ❏

My love opportunities – Mark 12:30-31
• God (loving enthusiastically – without reservation)    Better – Worse
1. With all my heart (warm, affectionate love)    ❏    ❏
2. With all my mind (intelligent, informed love)    ❏    ❏
3. With all my strength (energetic, devoted love)    ❏    ❏
4. With all my soul (integrated, holistic love)    ❏    ❏

• Others (loving empathetically – doing good, not harm)    Better – Worse

| | Better | Worse | | Better | Worse |
|---|---|---|---|---|---|
| 1. My mate | ❏ | ❏ | 5. My child | ❏ | ❏ |
| 2. My best friend | ❏ | ❏ | 6. My boss | ❏ | ❏ |
| 3. My co-worker | ❏ | ❏ | 7. My neighbor | ❏ | ❏ |
| 4. My enemy | ❏ | ❏ | 8. My encounters with strangers | ❏ | ❏ |

• Self (loving effectively – bringing out my best self)    Better – Worse
1. My body (caring for my physical needs and health)    ❏    ❏
2. My heart (caring for my emotional needs and self-esteem)    ❏    ❏
3. My mind (caring for my intellectual needs and growth)    ❏    ❏
4. My soul (caring for my spiritual needs and destiny)    ❏    ❏

### Sin Less          (Rate your progress this week)

• My sin snares (behaviors that make me LESS loving)    Better – Worse
1. Irrationality (unrealistic, unaware, untruthful)    ❏    ❏
2. Fabricating (exaggerating, demonizing, romanticizing)    ❏    ❏
3. Insensitivity (uncaring, unkind, unmindful)    ❏    ❏
4. Irresponsibility (undisciplined, unreliable, unaccountable)    ❏    ❏
• My sin challenges (ways I hurt the people I profess to love)   Better – Worse
1. Tongue (gossiping, criticizing, blaming, lying)    ❏    ❏
2. Temper (anger, negativity, intimidation)    ❏    ❏
3. Temptations (lust, pride, selfishness, laziness)    ❏    ❏

### My Loving Journal (developing my love-consciousness)
• I felt loved last week when …
• Loving choices I made last week:
• Unloving choices I made last week:
• This week I will love more by …
• This week I will sin less by …

# The Loving Mind

*"Whoever keeps His word, truly the love of God is*
*perfected in him." – 1 John 2:5*

It is impossible to live a life of love without faith in Jesus and His teaching. Abounding love is a consequence of a growing faith (2 Thessalonians 1:3); dwindling love is a sign of a shrinking faith. Chapter three will establish the unbreakable link between thinking biblically and loving effectively. Chapter four will explain the connection between unbelief and unloving behavior. The key to successful relationships is cultivating a loving mind (Philippians 2:5), and this is accomplished through believing and obeying the inspired Word of God.

# Chapter 3

# Love Clarified:
# Faith

*"Love must be as much a light as it is a flame."*
*– Henry David Thoreau*

---

The mind is God's remarkable creation. It enables humans to survive by learning how to control or adapt to their environment. It forms concepts about the way the world operates and permits people to live wisely and productively. However, the mind is incapable of knowing some things apart from divine revelation. Many spiritual, relational and eternal truths cannot be gleaned from experience alone.

Actually, the problem is not so much with the mind as with the faculties for gathering information by which it formulates ideas. Paul explained this phenomenon by saying, "[I]n the wisdom of God, the world through wisdom did not know God" (1 Corinthians 1:21). In other words, it appears that God intentionally equipped man with tools of perception (the five senses) that were limited in their ability to grasp certain aspects of reality. It was not that God intended to keep that knowledge to Himself, but that He intended to provide it at a time and in a way that suited a higher purpose. So how has God chosen to accomplish that end? The answer is – through faith!

## Faith and Natural Revelation

God has provided basic knowledge of Himself through what is called natural revelation – evidence of God that is accessible to human reasoning without the aid of Scripture or special revelation (Psalm 19:1). The brain responds favorably to natural revelation because it was spiritually formatted to do so.

The mind cannot be an entirely blank slate because some means of organizing sensory data is essential to form ideas. To use computer jargon, God has provided mankind with an operating system that enables him to process information. As part of that system, the Lord has installed an innate knowledge of His existence or a predisposition to believe in Him. By virtue of the way humans are made, they cannot help but contemplate their origin and conclude the reality of God when viewing the wonders of nature. Although pure spirit, His existence cannot be refuted by anyone who honestly examines the evidence at hand (Romans 1:19). Everything that can be touched, smelled or seen screams, "There is a God!" Yet one can override this intuitive response by repressing the truths communicated through the created order (Romans 1:18).

By observing nature, it is also possible to discern something about God's nature. Paul wrote, "[B]ecause what may be known of God is manifest in them, for God has shown it to them. For since the creation of the world His invisible attributes are clearly seen, being understood by the things that are made, even His eternal power and Godhead, so that they are without excuse" (Romans 1:19-20). Three traits are especially evident to unbiased onlookers:

• The immensity of the universe bears witness to the power of God.
• The complexity of the cosmos demonstrates the wisdom of God.
• The fertility of the earth attests to the love of God.

One who prepared a world so majestic and prolific must care deeply for those who inhabit it. God's compassionate character is on display through His creation, and His goodness calls forth love from the hearts of His people. Because they admire Him and worship Him, they strive to emulate Him by dealing generously and graciously with others.

Endeavoring to love as God does is like attempting to reproduce a painting by one of the great masters: Rembrandt, Monet or Picasso.

Although impossible to duplicate, it is the sincerest form of flattery. God helps Christians color their world by reproducing His love in the lives of all they meet. They make each day a masterpiece by applying brushstrokes of genuine imitation love!

## *Faith and Special Revelation*

• *Incarnation.* In addition to the proof of God that appears in nature, the Lord has provided supernatural confirmation of His existence. The most direct source of that knowledge was the incarnation of Jesus Christ. Moses' Law predicted Christ's coming and hinted at His compassion and selflessness. Yet when He arrived on earth, His life of love surpassed what was foretold (Colossians 2:17). So the Hebrews writer praised Jesus as the brightness of God's glory and the express image of His person (Hebrews 1:3).

When Philip asked Jesus to reveal the Father, the Lord replied, "He who has seen Me has seen the Father" (John 14:9). Therefore, one who desires to know God should look no further than Jesus (1:14-18; Colossians 1:15-19). And because God is love, one who desires to understand the meaning of love must also look to Christ. But how can a person know Him now that He has ascended to heaven?

• *Inspiration.* A secondary source of special revelation has been provided in the inspired Word of God. Scripture is the means God selected to provide humans with spiritual knowledge of which they can be absolutely certain. Jesus' appearance on earth was a temporary measure fulfilling a special purpose. The Bible is heaven's long-term provision of the information people need to live effectively and eternally.

Jesus explained, "Heaven and earth will pass away, but My words will by no means pass away" (Matthew 24:35). Peter added, "All flesh is as grass, and all the glory of man as the flower of the grass. The grass withers, and its flower falls away, but the word of the Lord endures forever. Now this is the word which by the gospel was preached to you" (1 Peter 1:24-25). This indestructible message provides the key to the love-based life.

As long as the world stands, the incorruptible life-giving Word will abide as a source of truth and wisdom (v. 23). Jesus was truth embodied (John 14:6), but the Bible is truth encoded (17:17). Jesus was wisdom incarnate (1 Corinthians 1:30), but the Bible is wisdom imprinted (2 Timothy 3:15). When the infallible Word of God is accurately translated and faithfully preached, Jesus is presented again to the mind with amazing results for those who embrace its message. So Paul exulted, "[I]t pleased God through the foolishness of the message preached to save those who believe" (1 Corinthians 1:21).

## The Sufficiency of Scripture

Although secondary and indirect as a source of knowledge, the gospel is more than sufficient to accomplish God's purpose of redeeming and renewing human hearts. That is because it is God's Word and not merely a vehicle of human communication. The qualitative difference between divine inspiration and human genius is astounding. Failure to appreciate the unique nature of the Bible deprives unbelievers of its wonderful benefits.

Jesus declared that His words were spirit and life (John 6:63). Paul affirmed Scripture to be God-breathed or inspired (2 Timothy 3:16). The Hebrews writer proclaimed that God's Word is "living and powerful, and sharper than any two-edged sword, piercing even to the division of soul and spirit, and of joints and marrow, and is a discerner of the thoughts and intents of the heart" (Hebrews 4:12). In other words, because it is completely true in every respect, it possesses thought-clarifying, life-enriching, soul-saving power. Nothing can change hearts and improve relationships like the Bible.

## Faith Activates the Word

But for the Word to have its proper effect, it must be activated by a believing mind (John 3:16; Romans 1:16). Jesus preached that faith as small as a mustard seed is capable of moving mountains (Matthew 17:20). Faith is the catalyst that releases the inherent power of the Word to bless the life and relationships of its recipient. The purpose of Christian belief is to prompt loving action. Without belief, one is not empowered to act. Belief sets things in motion. That is why proper beliefs are essential. Wrong beliefs prompt harmful action or inaction. True beliefs spur responsible, loving and healthful action. Fruitful relationships and productive lives are virtuous byproducts of a believing mind.

The writer of Hebrews provided a classic illustration of this principle (Hebrews 4:1-12). The Israelites who left Egypt perished in the wilderness before reaching their intended destination. What was the problem? Initially, the writer identified lack of faith as the difficulty (v. 2). Later, he mentioned disobedience as the cause (v. 6). Which was it? The correct answer is "both." Disobedience is a direct result of subscribing to the devil's misinformation. Failure to trust God inevitably leads to mistaken beliefs and misguided actions. The final result is a failure to love.

## *Walking by Faith*

Yet faith is not intrinsically beneficial. To be profitable it must be well placed. Faith that is not centered in Christ and His Word is reckless and destructive. The Bible alone is worthy of unreserved confidence as a knowledge source concerning Jesus Christ and authentic love (Romans 10:17). Belief in the reliability of Scripture motivates people to alter their lives by its teachings. The significance of faith is that it aligns the mind with life's realities and love's possibilities. Faith enables a Christian to see more clearly and, thereby, to live in greater harmony with the seen and unseen worlds. Conversely, those who reject the Bible operate on the basis of illusion and are out of step with the way life and relationships really work.

If Christians are commanded to "walk by faith and not by sight" (2 Corinthians 5:7), then faith must be superior to vision as a method of gaining insight to complete what is lacking in human understanding. Faith is the true missing link, the neglected cognitive tool by which reality is perceived and embraced. It is the sixth sense of the soul. Evolutionary science looks backward for connections with lesser creatures to explain mankind's roots, but the link of faith points upward to a loving Creator in whose image all humans have been made. Faith is no vestigial organ left over from a superstitious, unenlightened past. It is the spiritual counterpart of physical eyesight but with far greater advantages. Faith benefits both body and soul, and its blessings extend beyond time into eternity. A man born blind who possesses faith lives a far better life than a person with perfect vision who is never born again. Faith corrects faulty thinking and selfish living; therefore, it is a vital organ in the truest sense.

# Questions

1. What do you call the knowledge of God provided in creation?

2. What do you call the knowledge of God provided in Scripture?

3. What was the most direct source of knowledge about God?

4. What two terms did Jesus use to describe His words?

5. What releases the power of the Word in a person's life?

6. Where did Paul say faith originates?

7. With what does faith align the mind?

8. Faith is the spiritual counterpart of what physical sense?

9. On what basis do people operate after rejecting the Bible?

10. What is the missing link that explains man's origin and destiny?

# Discussion Questions

1. In what way is revelation superior to science and philosophy?

2. How is faith more important than physical eyesight?

3. Explain the relationship between faith and love.

# Love Quest Survey
## Pursuing a God-Shaped Heart

## Love More (Rate your progress this week)

My love skills (behaviors that make me MORE loving)    Better – Worse
1. Honesty (realistic, truthful, self-aware)    ❏    ❏
2. Empathy (thoughtful, compassionate, kind, forgiving)    ❏    ❏
3. Responsibility (accountable, reliable, disciplined)    ❏    ❏

My love opportunities – Mark 12:30-31
• God (loving enthusiastically – without reservation)    Better – Worse
1. With all my heart (warm, affectionate love)    ❏    ❏
2. With all my mind (intelligent, informed love)    ❏    ❏
3. With all my strength (energetic, devoted love)    ❏    ❏
4. With all my soul (integrated, holistic love)    ❏    ❏
• Others (loving empathetically – doing good, not harm)    Better – Worse
1. My mate    ❏    ❏    5. My child    ❏    ❏
2. My best friend    ❏    ❏    6. My boss    ❏    ❏
3. My co-worker    ❏    ❏    7. My neighbor    ❏    ❏
4. My enemy    ❏    ❏    8. My encounters    ❏    ❏
                              with strangers
• Self (loving effectively – bringing out my best self)    Better – Worse
1. My body (caring for my physical needs and health)    ❏    ❏
2. My heart (caring for my emotional needs and self-esteem)    ❏    ❏
3. My mind (caring for my intellectual needs and growth)    ❏    ❏
4. My soul (caring for my spiritual needs and destiny)    ❏    ❏

## Sin Less (Rate your progress this week)

• My sin snares (behaviors that make me LESS loving)    Better – Worse
1. Irrationality (unrealistic, unaware, untruthful)    ❏    ❏
2. Fabricating (exaggerating, demonizing, romanticizing)    ❏    ❏
3. Insensitivity (uncaring, unkind, unmindful)    ❏    ❏
4. Irresponsibility (undisciplined, unreliable, unaccountable)    ❏    ❏
• My sin challenges (ways I hurt the people I profess to love)    Better – Worse
1. Tongue (gossiping, criticizing, blaming, lying)    ❏    ❏
2. Temper (anger, negativity, intimidation)    ❏    ❏
3. Temptations (lust, pride, selfishness, laziness)    ❏    ❏

## My Loving Journal (developing my love-consciousness)
• I felt loved last week when …
• Loving choices I made last week:
• Unloving choices I made last week:
• This week I will love more by …
• This week I will sin less by …

*Chapter 4*

# *Love Confused:*
# Unbelief

*"Unbelief is blind." – John Milton*

---

S cientists once believed that the atom was the irreducible building
block from which all things were made. It is now well known that
subatomic particles such as quarks (constituents of protons and neu-
trons) underlie and explain the atomic order. In a similar way, those
who look at sin as the foundational explanation for evil fail to look at
the problem deep enough. Underlying sin is a misinformed mind. Sin,
therefore, is the byproduct or outworking of wrong beliefs.

That is not to say that sin is a purely intellectual problem without
moral implications. One can have access to correct information yet
choose not to accept or act upon it (2 Peter 3:5). Ignorance may be will-
ful, and misinformation may be self-imposed. In legal matters, deliberate ignorance is no better than reckless disregard for the law. The
same is true in spiritual matters (1 Peter 1:13). Those who break the
law of love are accountable, regardless of conscious intent.

## *The Selfish Mind*
Some wrongly held beliefs do not involve ethical or spiritual implications. For instance, if one believes that Louisville rather than

Frankfort is the capital of Kentucky, his mistaken belief is not rooted in selfishness. Untruths do not necessarily constitute a lie. Flawed facts do not automatically constitute a fib. Morality becomes an issue at the point where one's belief system is tainted by misguided self-interest.

An argument can be made that genuine self-interest is always healthy and positive and that those who truly promote their highest welfare are not guilty of sinful self-indulgence. It is when self-concern erodes into selfishness that it becomes destructive. Vanity is an unholy preoccupation with self that disregards the will of God and the well-being of others. However, the vainer one becomes, the more vigorously he will claim that his motives are disinterested and altruistic.

• *Sin and Self-Importance.* There is a vital connection between sin and self-importance that probably explains why pride is listed first in Solomon's list of the things God hates (Proverbs 6:16-19). Strangely, one can be totally blind to this self-absorption. The egotist deludes himself into believing that whatever serves his interests serves the interests of others. He equates his will with that of the Almighty. Vanity warps his worldview, twists his perception of truth, and damages his sense of community. Conceit causes one to behave in unloving and unlovely ways.

An arrogant person is self-confident to a fault. Warning against this tendency toward self-delusion, Jeremiah wrote, "The heart is deceitful above all things, and desperately wicked; who can know it?" (Jeremiah 17:9). Humans can always find a way to justify their unloving actions. That is why Solomon taught the value of self-doubt: "Trust in the LORD with all your heart, And lean not upon your own understanding" (Proverbs 3:5). Solomon was not condemning rational use of the mind or commending unsubstantiated faith; rather, he was lauding the worth of Scripture for informed, intelligent living. Where does a sound mind place its trust but in the Lord? And how does one trust in the Lord except through believing His revealed will?

• *Sin and Misplaced Trust.* Jesus taught that His words were mankind's only hope for happiness and heaven (Matthew 7:24-27; John 12:48). Likewise, His disciples taught that trusting the Savior's message was God's singular means for saving lost souls (2 Timothy 3:15; James 1:21). Respect for the power of Scripture does not diminish appreciation for Christ's atoning death or challenge His preeminent place in the hearts of His people. Rather than supplanting faith, the Word supplies faith in Christ. One could not know of Jesus' sacrifice without the testimony of inspired writers, nor could one know how to receive the blessings it made possible. To be strong in the Lord and in the power of His might, one must be strong in the gospel, for it is the power of God unto salvation. Confidence in Scripture is a matter of spiritual integrity, not a form of idolatry.

Pride and selfishness form the bedrock of unbelief. Unbelief is a term that describes the spiritual state of one living out of harmony with the will of God due to misplaced trust. It is the opposite of faith. Unbelief occurs when people distrust the Bible as the primary source of knowledge regarding life and love. It can also happen when they deny the truth or benefit of particular teachings (facts, commands and promises). In either case, it comes down to doubting or distorting the testimony of Scripture and failing to make use of available truth. When truth is treated as untruth, the unbeliever's conduct in life and preparations for eternity are based on mistaken beliefs. The harmful effects of this disbelief are chilling (Mark 16:16).

## *The Darkened Mind*

Few things in life are more terrifying than darkness. Without a light to guide them, travelers grope and stumble through the gloom. The same is true for those who attempt to make their way through life without the illumination of the Bible (Psalm 119:105). Their path is marked by two phantoms of the imagination: fear and fantasy. The first causes needless anxiety (worry); the second causes impracticality (wishful thinking). The result of irrational thinking is dysfunctional living.

In his letter to the Romans, Paul explained what he witnessed when men and women go through life without grateful recognition of their Creator: they "became futile in their thoughts, and their foolish hearts were darkened" (Romans 1:21). The letter to the Ephesians contains similar words describing the lives of unbelieving Gentiles.

> This I say, therefore, and testify in the Lord, that you should no longer walk as the rest of the Gentiles walk, in the futility of their mind, having their understanding darkened, being

alienated from the life of God, because of the ignorance that is in them, because of the blindness of their heart; who, being past feeling, have given themselves over to lewdness, to work all uncleanliness with greediness (Ephesians 4:17-19).

Sin begins in a darkened mind. Paul equated this heart condition with four unflattering characteristics:
- Past feeling – Callousness (lack of compassion)
- Blindness – Obliviousness (lack of consciousness)
- Ignorance – Shallowness (lack of comprehension)
- Futility – Unfruitfulness (lack of contribution)

The word "futile" (vain or empty) indicates that such thinking is unproductive of good and unregulated by godly goals. Such a person may be resolutely set on doing evil. In his clouded thinking, the end justifies his heartless means. The Hamans, Herods and Hitlers of the world fall into this category.

Conversely, life may be driven by momentary lusts and is robbed of any higher purpose. Whims and cravings dominate this lifestyle. Moral sensibility is lost, alienation replaces fellowship, and death supplants life when one lives for self. Only lewdness, uncleanliness and greediness remain as a result. It is a revolting description of a life lived without regard for anyone but self. A darkened mind is one in which the light of love has gone out.

## Truth Is Like Light

In contrast, Jesus is the light of the world by virtue of His example and teaching. He came to bring life and immortality to light and dispel the dark thinking that robs human existence of meaning and joy. Those who receive Jesus' teaching are brought out of life's shadows into the marvelous light of a loving life (1 Peter 2:9; Colossians 1:13). Disciples who love Jesus and learn from Him are committed to continuing the Lord's mission by serving as light bearers in a sin-darkened world (Philippians 2:14-16; Matthew 5:14-16). They spend their remaining days on earth rescuing others from beliefs and judgments that are delusional and self-destructive.

Paul described this commitment to truth-awareness as a family characteristic: "But you, brethren, are not in darkness, so that this Day should overtake you as a thief. You are all sons of light and sons of the day. We are not of the night nor of darkness" (1 Thessalonians 5:4-5). Because God is light, those who call Him Father must be children of light (1 John 1:5). Nevertheless, maintaining a life devoted to life, light and love is a continuing struggle for every Christian.

## *Truth Is Like Armor*

The struggle is so great, in fact, that the Bible describes it as war: "For the weapons of our warfare are not carnal but mighty in God for pulling down strongholds, casting down arguments and every high thing that exalts itself against the knowledge of God, bringing every thought into captivity to the obedience of Christ" (2 Corinthians 10:4-5). Just as cultures clash, so good and evil vie for the high ground of the human heart to determine which beliefs and values will reign.

• *Unseating Error.* Because wrong beliefs are deeply entrenched, they are called the stronghold of Satan. Just as an army besieges a city or soldiers assail a bunker, so Christians must root out thoughts that subvert biblical teaching and spiritual values. Like the removal of a defiant and abusive dictator, arguments that contradict truth must be cast down. Rogue thoughts must be brought into captivity to Christ in the way that a conquering army restores peace to a country whose totalitarian regime has been overthrown.

It was in this connection that Jesus declared, "[Y]ou shall know the truth, and the truth shall make you free" (John 8:32). Jesus understood that believing what is false leaves a person stuck until he changes the thinking that dictates his actions. True beliefs free us from self-defeating behavior. False beliefs ensnare people in conflict and confusion. Dysfunction, division and damnation are the fruits of failed thinking.

• *Perfecting Knowledge.* Bringing thought into captivity to Christ does not restrict knowledge but rather perfects it. Jesus' teaching reconnects minds with reality and releases them from imprisonment to unloving thoughts that produce hurtful actions. Christ's followers are freed from sinful patterns of behavior and the suffering they produce, both temporally and eternally. In contrast, Satan is busy perpetuating lies that lead to unnecessary antagonism. He is rightly called the "evil one" because he convinces people they are behaving responsibly and compassionately when they are inflicting pointless pain in the lives of those around them. What worse form of captivity could there be?

As Christians prepare to fight their daily battle against the devil's deceit, Paul urges them to put on the armor of God (Ephesians 6:10-17). Although this analogy is a familiar one, readers often fail to see that each piece of armor is an element of a sound Christian belief system. If the fight is for the mind, the armor must be related to the mind as well. Each piece – the belt, breastplate, shoes, shield and helmet – describes a way of thinking that determines the way a person interacts with the surrounding world. To defeat Satan one must be staunchly devoted to five beliefs:

- Honesty is better than deception.
- Right is better than wrong.
- Peace is better than conflict.
- Faith is better than unbelief.
- Hope is better than despair.

These traits are critical components of a loving mindset. When any of these items are missing, a victorious life is not possible. To love well, a person must be candid, conscientious, conciliatory, confident and composed.

Paul continued his illustration by comparing the Word of God to a sword. Like its physical counterpart, it can be used defensively to ward off destructive beliefs or offensively to retake hearts that have succumbed to mistaken beliefs. Truth is a liberator from wrong thinking and its harmful consequences.

## *Truth Is Like Rain*

In a less dramatic but more charming analogy, Isaiah compared truth to life-sustaining rain.

> For as the rain comes down, and the snow from heaven, and do not return there, but water the earth, and make it bring forth and bud, that it may give seed to the sower and bread to the eater, so shall My word be that goes forth from My mouth; it shall not return to Me void, but it shall accomplish

what I please, and it shall prosper in the thing for which I sent it (Isaiah 55:10-11).

Like rain, truth "brings forth." And like water, it can take many forms: it can be personified, preached or put down on paper. The medium of its conveyance is not as critical as its effect upon lives. It can be words on a page or fire in the bones, but whenever and however it is encountered, God's Word evokes a human response. Truth releases a person's spiritual potential just as water and light call forth life from dormant seeds. Blossoming relationships and fruitful lives are evidence of the soul's acquaintance with truth.

## *The Greatest Truth*

Perhaps the hardest of all truths to accept is "God loves me." When Adam and Eve sinned, it was because Satan convinced them God could not possibly be as trustworthy and caring as He appeared. When the Israelites turned their hearts back to Egypt, it was because they doubted God's dedication and ability to meet their needs. Despite their personal experience with God's unfailing love, He simply seemed too good to be true.

So today, people struggle with whether to believe in a Father whose love, wisdom and power are infinite and wholly devoted to their well-being. In turn, they must decide whether to bring their thoughts and lives under the authority of His inspired Word. Those who trust God will not be disappointed. They will discover that the Bible restores soundness to the mind and health to relationships. Like armor, it protects. Like light, it guides. Like rain, it nourishes. Believe it and begin enjoying the rich relationships and bountiful blessings truth affords!

## *Questions*

1. What is vanity?

2. What did Solomon say not to lean upon?

3. What did Jesus bring to light (2 Timothy 1:10)?

4. To what did Paul compare wrong beliefs (2 Corinthians 10:4-5)?

5. To what did Paul compare right beliefs (Ephesians 6:10-20)?

6. To what did Isaiah compare God's truth (Isaiah 55:10-11)?

7. How is God's Word like light?

8. How is God's Word like armor?

9. How is God's Word like rain?

10. What is one of the hardest of all truths to believe?

## *Discussion Questions*

1. Is unbelief an intellectual or moral problem?

2. How does the heart deceive, and what is the solution to this problem?

3. What did Jesus mean when He said that truth sets us free?

# Love Quest Survey
## Pursuing a God-Shaped Heart

## Love More            (Rate your progress this week)

My love skills (behaviors that make me MORE loving)    Better – Worse

| | Better | Worse |
|---|---|---|
| 1. Honesty (realistic, truthful, self-aware) | ❏ | ❏ |
| 2. Empathy (thoughtful, compassionate, kind, forgiving) | ❏ | ❏ |
| 3. Responsibility (accountable, reliable, disciplined) | ❏ | ❏ |

My love opportunities – Mark 12:30-31

• God (loving enthusiastically – without reservation)    Better – Worse

| | Better | Worse |
|---|---|---|
| 1. With all my heart (warm, affectionate love) | ❏ | ❏ |
| 2. With all my mind (intelligent, informed love) | ❏ | ❏ |
| 3. With all my strength (energetic, devoted love) | ❏ | ❏ |
| 4. With all my soul (integrated, holistic love) | ❏ | ❏ |

• Others (loving empathetically – doing good, not harm)    Better – Worse

| | Better | Worse | | Better | Worse |
|---|---|---|---|---|---|
| 1. My mate | ❏ | ❏ | 5. My child | ❏ | ❏ |
| 2. My best friend | ❏ | ❏ | 6. My boss | ❏ | ❏ |
| 3. My co-worker | ❏ | ❏ | 7. My neighbor | ❏ | ❏ |
| 4. My enemy | ❏ | ❏ | 8. My encounters with strangers | ❏ | ❏ |

• Self (loving effectively – bringing out my best self)    Better – Worse

| | Better | Worse |
|---|---|---|
| 1. My body (caring for my physical needs and health) | ❏ | ❏ |
| 2. My heart (caring for my emotional needs and self-esteem) | ❏ | ❏ |
| 3. My mind (caring for my intellectual needs and growth) | ❏ | ❏ |
| 4. My soul (caring for my spiritual needs and destiny) | ❏ | ❏ |

## Sin Less            (Rate your progress this week)

• My sin snares (behaviors that make me LESS loving)    Better – Worse

| | Better | Worse |
|---|---|---|
| 1. Irrationality (unrealistic, unaware, untruthful) | ❏ | ❏ |
| 2. Fabricating (exaggerating, demonizing, romanticizing) | ❏ | ❏ |
| 3. Insensitivity (uncaring, unkind, unmindful) | ❏ | ❏ |
| 4. Irresponsibility (undisciplined, unreliable, unaccountable) | ❏ | ❏ |

• My sin challenges (ways I hurt the people I profess to love) Better – Worse

| | Better | Worse |
|---|---|---|
| 1. Tongue (gossiping, criticizing, blaming, lying) | ❏ | ❏ |
| 2. Temper (anger, negativity, intimidation) | ❏ | ❏ |
| 3. Temptations (lust, pride, selfishness, laziness) | ❏ | ❏ |

## My Loving Journal (developing my love-consciousness)

• I felt loved last week when …
• Loving choices I made last week:
• Unloving choices I made last week:
• This week I will love more by …
• This week I will sin less by …

# The Loving Choice

*"Let all that you do be done with love." – 1 Corinthians 16:14*

---

L ove is more than a pleasant emotion. In fact, love often begins when one least feels like loving. At that moment, a painful inward change must occur for the relationship to continue. Without sacrifice or stretching, there is no room for another person in one's life. In chapter five we learn that repentance is making room for others in a sin-crowded heart. In chapter six we see that salvation is freedom from unloving choices and a self-centered heart. The common element in repentance and salvation is the choice to love more and sin less. No decision will be more important in your lifetime.

# Chapter 5

# *Love Redirected:*
# Repentance

*"Repentance is another name for aspiration."*
*– Henry Ward Beecher*

---

Hydrogen and oxygen are noteworthy elements in their own right, but together, they make something wholly new and wonderful – water! This marvel of the chemical world has its parallel in the spiritual realm. Faith and repentance are valuable elements of the spiritual life, but when they are combined, their true power for good is realized.

## Repentance Completes Faith

Mere mental assent is an inadequate response to the saving work of Christ upon the cross. Correct beliefs, good intentions and pious words without corresponding behavior is the spiritual equivalent of a human corpse (James 2:14-26). A corpse is a body lacking an animating spirit. When a person is alive, there are vital signs that demonstrate the presence of a lifeforce. Similarly, when faith is alive, its vitality is verified by acts of love seen in good works (Hebrews 10:24).

Just as water requires two parts hydrogen to one part oxygen, so faith is the principal part of an appropriate human response to the gospel. Still, unless faith is fused with repentance, there is no remission of sins. "Faith" that does not change one's life cannot alter one's destiny.

## Repentance Requires Resolve

If faith excludes will, it is merely intellectual and incapable of accomplishing God's aims. It is best illustrated by the way demons responded to Christ (Mark 1:21-24). They knew He was the Holy One of God, yet they saw Him as an enemy to be feared and resisted. Their knowledge of Christ was partially correct – they knew He was divine and powerful – yet something was desperately wrong with their grasp of His purpose and mission. Like demons, many people concede God's existence but do not embrace Him in love. Like demons, they resist His will and behave in ways that are self-destructive and harmful to others.

Repentance also involves the exercise of free will. Faith is the positive side of conversion to Christ. Repentance views the same experience from a slightly different angle. Faith is embracing Christ; repentance is letting go of sin. However, the letting go is always purposeful because the ultimate aim is to lay hold of Christ. Both involve a choice that changes the direction of one's life.

When an EMT arrives on an accident scene and cannot find a victim's pulse, he may attempt to revive the heart. Repentance is resuscitation of the spiritual heart. The difference is that physical revival is involuntary and can occur even if the person being treated is unconscious. Spiritual revival cannot happen this way because thinking and purposing are essential. Although others may help, the real work must be done by the patient himself. Unless there is a will to live and a willingness to change, hope is lost. But no one is beyond healing who clings to the desire for a healthier life. Fundamental to spiritual recovery is the determination to live and to love better.

Repentance is always a matter of life and death. Failure to repent can mean the death of a soul, valued friendships or human potential. Conversely, choosing to repent means that unloving habits and attitudes must be crucified. To become a new man, the old man must die. If the old man does not die, the new man cannot live.

## Repentance Produces Wholeheartedness

Lot's wife is a tragic example of one whose faith was not completed by repentance. When God's messengers came to warn of Sodom's coming destruction, she and her family were slow to flee. Sympathetic angels took them by the hand to rescue them from disaster. Although Lot's wife knew devastation was coming, she failed to rid her heart of its longing for the sinful city. When delay resulted in death, she became the classic symbol of indecision (Genesis 19).

Those who hesitate while their souls' safety hangs in the balance are repeating the error of Lot's wife. God provides both opportunity and encouragement to escape the consequences of sin, but halfhearted believers vacillate until the moment of decision has passed. To embrace a new future, one must be willing to let go of the past. Some habits, attitudes and relationships must be relinquished to experience renewal. It all comes down to a choice of the heart.

It is impossible to leave sin halfway. Looking backward is not merely awkward and dangerous, it is deadly. Sin will overtake a person every time he clings to it. He cannot escape what he carries with him in his heart. When he succumbs to sin, he will not be the same person as before. Like Lot's wife, he will be hardened by the experience.

Attempts to flee sin without forsaking the desire to sin are nothing more than flights of fancy. To leave sin behind, one must stop loving it. As a consequence, the real question must be, "How do I stop loving sin?" The answer is to kill it. Love for sin is defeated by developing a greater love for something better.

## *Repentance Improves Life*

To embrace a new, healthier, more positive future, it is necessary to make a break with the behaviors that hold one back in life. Uncommitted Christians want to have their cake and eat it too. They believe they can enjoy success without sacrifice. Wise people know this is impossible. You cannot abuse your body with addictive substances and enjoy good health. You cannot spend recklessly and remain financially solvent. People complain about their circumstances, but most can be traced back to their own decisions. They view themselves as victims of God's neglect or of cruel fate, but in reality, they have reaped what they have sown.

Repentance, then, should not be seen as giving up what is valuable, but releasing what hinders a person from experiencing health, holiness and happiness.

• It is not foregoing joy until Jesus returns but redefining joy.

• It is not sacrificing all pleasure but discarding worldly concepts of pleasure.
• The result is not less life but more life and more love.

A cluttered room must be cleaned to make room for a guest. That means trash and useless items must be removed if the visitor is to feel welcome. Getting ready for company is a demanding task, but love turns the drudgery into pure joy. Similarly, repentance is removing the junk from one's life to prepare for sacred company. To receive Christ, sin must go. To make room for others, selfishness must go. Whatever habits and attitudes are abandoned, the joy of intimacy will more than replace. The pain of change will shortly give way to deep and abiding satisfaction.

When remodeling a house, it is helpful to ask, "What is not working?" When renovating your life, it is good to ask, "What needs to go?" For instance, a person in a treasured but troubled relationship might inquire, "What am I clinging to that is keeping this relationship from its potential?" When you find the answer, start heading for the dumpster (Philippians 3:7-8). Do not throw out your faith and do not abandon your values, but be ready to relinquish whatever is worthless or of lesser value than the relationship. When the rubbish goes, the relationship grows!

## *Repentance Demands Honesty*

Motivation for repentance comes from assessing life's circumstances and possibilities with total honesty. Continuation in sin is rooted in denial or self-deceit. Conversion occurs when people quit kidding themselves about the hurt their sins have caused others and come clean about the unhappiness it has brought into their own lives.

When people get fed up with sin's effects and begin searching for better answers, they are prime candidates for a life-changing encounter with the gospel of Christ. The loveliness of Jesus' life has a drawing power that pulls penitent hearts His direction. Those who embrace the Lord in faith are ready to submit to His leadership and are eager to order their lives by His teaching and example. Faith is aligning the mind with Jesus' mind; repentance is aligning the will with Jesus' will.

Obedience is the end result of this process. It is configuring words and deeds with biblical truth and life's realities. Compliance begins initially with baptism and is evident thereafter in worship and service to God. Nowhere, however, is the fruit of repentance more obvious than in one's relationships.

## Repentance Revives Relationships

The relational nature of repentance can be illustrated by Mark's account of the man Jesus healed in the region of the Gadarenes (Mark 5:1-15). Legion's erratic behavior caused him to live apart from the townspeople in the mountains and tombs. The consequence of demonic possession was unfitness to live around other people. His bizarre behavior caused him to frighten and injure others. When Jesus expelled the evil spirits and restored the man to his right mind, he was also restored to a new condition of sociability.

Today, those who surrender their minds to Satan's control manifest an incivility that surfaces in many forms. On the mild side, distorted thinking leads to coarseness, vulgarity, disrespect and selfishness. On the harsh side, worldly wisdom produces gossip, slander, abusiveness and violence. Although sinful ways of interacting with others never achieve the desired end, the tendency is to intensify the offensive behaviors rather than correct the faulty beliefs. Invariably, the result is even greater alienation.

When people repent of sin, they relate more effectively with the people God brings into their lives. They long to serve and support them rather than use or undermine them. They want to encourage and edify rather than discourage and devastate. Faith in Christ makes one aware of improved ways of relating to others. Repentance removes the causes of estrangement and leads people to adopt methods that can strengthen their relationships.

Repentance is a spiritual tool for repositioning your heart and reinventing your circumstances. The consequence of conversion is a life of unbounded love. Marriages are mended, and homes are healed. Neighbors become nicer, and workers become worthy of their hire. Repentance is the renewal of responsible love.

# Questions

1. How did James describe faith without accompanying works?

2. What image did James use to depict faith without works?

3. When faith is alive, what can one expect to see?

4. Who did demons say Jesus was?

5. What did the demons fail to do?

6. What is the word for aligning your mind with God's mind?

7. What is the word for aligning your will with God's will?

8. What follows faith and repentance?

9. Where is the fruit of repentance most obvious?

10. What was the name of the demon-possessed man Jesus healed?

# Discussion Questions

1. How is repentance a form of aspiration?

2. Why is repentance relational?

3. What is the relationship between honesty and repentance?

# Love Quest Survey
## Pursuing a God-Shaped Heart

## Love More      (Rate your progress this week)

My love skills (behaviors that make me MORE loving)    Better – Worse
1. Honesty (realistic, truthful, self-aware)     ❑    ❑
2. Empathy (thoughtful, compassionate, kind, forgiving)   ❑    ❑
3. Responsibility (accountable, reliable, disciplined)   ❑    ❑

My love opportunities – Mark 12:30-31
• God (loving enthusiastically – without reservation)    Better – Worse
1. With all my heart (warm, affectionate love)    ❑    ❑
2. With all my mind (intelligent, informed love)    ❑    ❑
3. With all my strength (energetic, devoted love)    ❑    ❑
4. With all my soul (integrated, holistic love)    ❑    ❑
• Others (loving empathetically – doing good, not harm)   Better – Worse

| | Better | Worse | | Better | Worse |
|---|---|---|---|---|---|
| 1. My mate | ❑ | ❑ | 5. My child | ❑ | ❑ |
| 2. My best friend | ❑ | ❑ | 6. My boss | ❑ | ❑ |
| 3. My co-worker | ❑ | ❑ | 7. My neighbor | ❑ | ❑ |
| 4. My enemy | ❑ | ❑ | 8. My encounters with strangers | ❑ | ❑ |

• Self (loving effectively – bringing out my best self)   Better – Worse
1. My body (caring for my physical needs and health)   ❑    ❑
2. My heart (caring for my emotional needs and self-esteem)   ❑    ❑
3. My mind (caring for my intellectual needs and growth)   ❑    ❑
4. My soul (caring for my spiritual needs and destiny)   ❑    ❑

## Sin Less      (Rate your progress this week)

• My sin snares (behaviors that make me LESS loving)   Better – Worse
1. Irrationality (unrealistic, unaware, untruthful)   ❑    ❑
2. Fabricating (exaggerating, demonizing, romanticizing)   ❑    ❑
3. Insensitivity (uncaring, unkind, unmindful)   ❑    ❑
4. Irresponsibility (undisciplined, unreliable, unaccountable)   ❑    ❑
• My sin challenges (ways I hurt the people I profess to love) Better – Worse
1. Tongue (gossiping, criticizing, blaming, lying)   ❑    ❑
2. Temper (anger, negativity, intimidation)   ❑    ❑
3. Temptations (lust, pride, selfishness, laziness)   ❑    ❑

## My Loving Journal (developing my love-consciousness)
• I felt loved last week when …
• Loving choices I made last week:
• Unloving choices I made last week:
• This week I will love more by …
• This week I will sin less by …

# Chapter 6

# *Love Rescued:*
# Salvation

> *"Three things are necessary for the salvation of man: to know what he ought to believe; to know what he ought to desire; and to know what he ought to do."* – Thomas Aquinas

I f a top-10 list was compiled of the most precious words in the world, no doubt "salvation" would make the cut. This bold term refers to being rescued from something ominous and evil – but from what? To answer, "sin" does not sufficiently clarify the issue. Going one step further and defining sin as unloving thoughts, words and deeds sheds new light on the subject. It demystifies the concept and provides additional incentive for holy living. One who grasps the deeper meaning of salvation is better prepared to dispense with sin and pursue a life of love.

## *Components of Conversion*
• *Hearing.* Every component of conversion plays a critical role in the salvation process. For instance, salvation begins with hearing the Word of God (Romans 10:14-15). Hearing is vital to salvation because one cannot be delivered from the effects of wrong beliefs without coming in contact with information to correct those beliefs. Or as Jesus put it, "[Y]ou shall know the truth, and the truth shall make you free" (John 8:32). Truth liberates believers from bondage to sin by freeing them from misguided notions that enslave them in self-defeating behavior.

God's Word is the truth that saves (2 Timothy 3:15), but truth that is not delivered or received cannot have its intended effect. The mind must get in touch with truth to be rescued from error. The most fundamental of all truths is that God is love. Other truths grow out of this foundational concept and find their meaning in it. Apart from this truth, nothing else could possibly matter.

• *Believing.* Possessing correct information is vital to salvation, but it by no means guarantees deliverance from sin. Truth that is unwelcome cannot do its work. Embracing truth is the key to receiving its benefits (Mark 16:16). Though humans are incapable of possessing infinite truth, they can embrace the One who personifies all truth (John 14:6). In other words, salvation does not require omniscience, but it does call for faith.

Consider this medical analogy: when a person becomes ill, it is not necessary to go to medical school to be healed, but it is advisable to go to a doctor. However, a patient who lacks confidence in his doctor will not follow his treatment. Similarly, one who lacks faith in Jesus (the Great Physician) will not follow His instructions and cannot receive the benefits they were intended to provide (Luke 6:46). Therefore, trusting Jesus is the cure for sin and its relational ills.

• *Repenting.* People who know what is right but are unwilling to change cannot be delivered from their destructive ways. That is why repentance is essential to enjoy spiritual renewal. In repentance, a believer admits the hurtfulness and futility of his pre-conversion lifestyle, particularly in the realm of relationships. The believer also purposes to mend those relationships by modifying behavior in keeping with Christ's example and teaching. Before conversion, interaction with others is typified by flawed attempts to meet one's own needs. Post-conversion associations are characterized by a desire to help others grow and maximize their potential as God's creatures. The focus shifts from my wants to others' needs, and surprisingly, my needs are met in caring for others.

• *Confessing.* In confession, a believer is saved from self-absorption by acknowledging the perfection of Christ as a divine role model for improved relationships (Romans 10:10). The goal of Christianity is not to be religious but to love better. The focus is not on rules – although rules are a necessary and beneficial part of community life – but on people. When a person confesses that Jesus is the Christ, the Son of the Living God, he declares his confidence that Christ is the only one capable of dealing with the selfishness that plagued his former relationships. He proclaims that Jesus is not only his Maker and Messiah, but also his Mentor for relating to others in the best possible way.

• *Baptism.* When a person is baptized into Jesus Christ, he not only expresses love for the Lord, but he also seals a bond committing himself to love as the Lord does (Galatians 3:27). Those who have been immersed in Jesus' love are committed to sharing that experience with others. Practicing and promoting love becomes the ultimate purpose of life and nothing is more joyful than fulfilling this mission. Everyday becomes an adventure as Christians watch for opportunities to imitate Christ by caring for the needs of those around them.

Conversion is a revolution of the heart, and love is its liberator. Love reaches the heart through hearing, resonates in the heart through believing, redirects the heart though repenting, reaffirms the heart through confession, and recommits the heart through baptism. When love is restored to its rightful place, the soul is refreshed and relationships are revitalized (Acts 3:19).

## *Synonyms for Salvation*

The Bible presents many synonyms for salvation in Christ, but each is connected by a common thread. As several of these terms are presented, be on the lookout for the unifying principle underlying them all.

• *Reconciliation.* The first synonym to consider is "reconciliation" (2 Corinthians 5:18-19). To reconcile means to reunite friends who have become estranged. It implies a rift caused by sin, but emphasizes the gladness of coming together again. The restoration of former ties is not forced or unpleasant; reconciliation suggests joyous association. It hints at the reinstatement of warm affectionate bonds.

• *Adoption.* "Adoption" is a familial metaphor for what takes place in conversion (Galatians 4:4-7). Through the process of adoption, a person outside of a family is granted all the rights and privileges that belong to one who is born into the family. The change in legal status is not only recognized by the father but by siblings as well. So a

Christian, by virtue of the birth in water and Spirit, becomes part of God's household and a member of the community of faith. The new convert is immersed not only in God's love but also the love of faithful brethren. As he experiences the meaning of salvation in Christ, it becomes his responsibility to reach out to others with the message of a loving family with room in their hearts for another adopted child.

• *Redemption.* "Redemption" is another word for salvation that conveys a change in status (Ephesians 1:7). When people allow Satan to control their thoughts, they become slaves to the deceiver, as well as to their own desires. The result is bondage of the worst kind. Christ's blood was shed to purchase the freedom of those held captive to egotism, ill will and insensitivity. Christians serve a new Lord who genuinely cares for their happiness and well-being. The redeemed express their gratitude by reflecting His loving nature in their own lives. As bondservants of the Prince of Peace, they promote harmony over hatred and concord over conflict.

• *Propitiation.* "Propitiation" suggests payment of a different kind. In this case, the payment is to satisfy an offended party (Romans 3:23-26). Every sin is an offense against God because, as Father of all injured parties, He feels the pain of every person who is sinned against. His anger at the mistreatment of His children is righteous rather than prejudicial. His holiness will not allow Him to ignore or minimize the offender's sin. Propitiation recognizes the seriousness of sin as a relational offense that must be appeased and corrected. Yet it also exults in the forgiveness of the offender who is penitent and determined to do better in the future.

• *Regeneration.* Salvation can also be referred to as "regeneration" (Titus 3:5). A saved person is one who partakes in new life through a process requiring the end of an old life (Galatians 5:24). Paul said that when a person emerges from the watery grave of baptism, he rises to "walk in newness of life" (Romans 6:4). New Christians are not the same people, only wetter; they think differently, speak differently, feel differently and act differently. Most of all, they relate differently. Their new life is not theirs but Christ's who lives in them. It is a life characterized by a hatred for hostility and fervor for fellowship.

## The Focus of Forgiveness

Our list of words linked to salvation puts the picture of forgiveness in clearer focus. Each one expresses the relational nature of Christ's saving work. Salvation is a positive change in one's relationship with God that enables a constructive change in one's relationship with others. That change begins when a person accepts God's love and the offering of His Son for the forgiveness of sin. It continues in a readiness to lay down one's own life in loving service to others. When believers renounce their former lives based on mistaken beliefs about love, they enter a doorway to abundant and everlasting life.

The focal point of Christ's work of atonement was the shedding of His blood. Contacting Jesus' blood is essential to God's plan of salvation (1 Peter 1:18; Revelation 1:5; Hebrews 10:22; Romans 6:3). Precisely how the blood works is a mystery, but the power of Jesus' blood is undeniable. Nothing is better than Jesus' sacrificial love for motivating people to embark on a journey of personal transformation. When Jesus loved, He held nothing back: not His time, His energy or His possessions. And yet He gave more. Jesus gave not only His heart, but also the very blood coursing through His veins. Jesus' blood brings love into focus as nothing else can.

## The Goal of Salvation

Salvation is both *from* something and *to* something. It is liberation from a selfishness that leads to estrangement from God and alienation from man. It is also deliverance from the outpouring of God's wrath that awaits those who do not repent of their unloving ways. Those who cannot envision a literal hell with eternal flames underestimate the awfulness of sin and God's hatred for it. Still, apart from physical pain, eternity will be filled with unpleasantness for those who cling to their sins. It will mean separation from all who are loving, merciful and kind to dwell forever with those who are hateful, vindictive and cruel. It will mean the end of peace and contentment and the beginning of endless suffering and regret.

While residents of hell pass their time in weeping and gnashing of teeth, citizens of heaven engage in joyous banqueting. The saved will take pleasure in uninterrupted fellowship with the redeemed and unhindered access to God. The light of love will never fail to shine there. More blessed than beautiful buildings, transformed bodies and infinite resources are the perfected relationships that abound in glory. Heaven is first and foremost a place of love – untainted, unending, unfathomable love.

## *Rescued Priorities*

When Adam and Eve sinned, death became a part of human experience. When Jesus died at Calvary, the remedy to death was offered to mankind. Salvation reverses the effects of Adam's sin by enriching the present life with all the redemptive blessings available in Christ (Ephesians 1:3). The chief of those blessings is the return of love to the pinnacle of one's priorities.

Salvation also stretches into eternity by enlarging one's hope of life hereafter. That hope entails freedom from future punishment for unloving acts of the past. It also includes joyful anticipation of an existence free from the presence and power of sin.

Until Jesus returns, Christians are to provide earth's populace with a small sample of the happiness that awaits those who have been washed in the blood of the Lamb. The believer's mission is to model Christ's love by flooding the earth with good news and good deeds. The goal is to restore health to relationships suffering from the shortage of love known as sin. Without salvation, intimacy of this kind is impossible, but with God's love, all things are possible.

## *Questions*

1. Define "salvation."

2. What is the goal of salvation?

3. What word for salvation refers to restoring friendship?

4. What word for salvation involves a family metaphor?

5. What word for salvation employs a slave analogy?

6. What word for forgiveness refers to satisfying an offended party?

7. What word for salvation indicates partaking of new life?

8. What do these synonyms or analogies have in common?

9. From what preeminent vice does Christ save a person?

10. To what preeminent virtue does Christ save a person?

11. Salvation reverses the effects of whose sin?

## *Discussion Questions*

1. Explain whether salvation is a condition or a destination.

2. What benefits of salvation are you enjoying today?

3. What will salvation be like in heaven?

# Love Quest Survey
## Pursuing a God-Shaped Heart

### Love More      (Rate your progress this week)

My love skills (behaviors that make me MORE loving)    Better – Worse

| | Better | Worse |
|---|---|---|
| 1. Honesty (realistic, truthful, self-aware) | ❏ | ❏ |
| 2. Empathy (thoughtful, compassionate, kind, forgiving) | ❏ | ❏ |
| 3. Responsibility (accountable, reliable, disciplined) | ❏ | ❏ |

My love opportunities – Mark 12:30-31

• God (loving enthusiastically – without reservation)    Better – Worse

| | Better | Worse |
|---|---|---|
| 1. With all my heart (warm, affectionate love) | ❏ | ❏ |
| 2. With all my mind (intelligent, informed love) | ❏ | ❏ |
| 3. With all my strength (energetic, devoted love) | ❏ | ❏ |
| 4. With all my soul (integrated, holistic love) | ❏ | ❏ |

• Others (loving empathetically – doing good, not harm)    Better – Worse

| | Better | Worse | | Better | Worse |
|---|---|---|---|---|---|
| 1. My mate | ❏ | ❏ | 5. My child | ❏ | ❏ |
| 2. My best friend | ❏ | ❏ | 6. My boss | ❏ | ❏ |
| 3. My co-worker | ❏ | ❏ | 7. My neighbor | ❏ | ❏ |
| 4. My enemy | ❏ | ❏ | 8. My encounters with strangers | ❏ | ❏ |

• Self (loving effectively – bringing out my best self)    Better – Worse

| | Better | Worse |
|---|---|---|
| 1. My body (caring for my physical needs and health) | ❏ | ❏ |
| 2. My heart (caring for my emotional needs and self-esteem) | ❏ | ❏ |
| 3. My mind (caring for my intellectual needs and growth) | ❏ | ❏ |
| 4. My soul (caring for my spiritual needs and destiny) | ❏ | ❏ |

### Sin Less      (Rate your progress this week)

• My sin snares (behaviors that make me LESS loving)    Better – Worse

| | Better | Worse |
|---|---|---|
| 1. Irrationality (unrealistic, unaware, untruthful) | ❏ | ❏ |
| 2. Fabricating (exaggerating, demonizing, romanticizing) | ❏ | ❏ |
| 3. Insensitivity (uncaring, unkind, unmindful) | ❏ | ❏ |
| 4. Irresponsibility (undisciplined, unreliable, unaccountable) | ❏ | ❏ |

• My sin challenges (ways I hurt the people I profess to love) Better – Worse

| | Better | Worse |
|---|---|---|
| 1. Tongue (gossiping, criticizing, blaming, lying) | ❏ | ❏ |
| 2. Temper (anger, negativity, intimidation) | ❏ | ❏ |
| 3. Temptations (lust, pride, selfishness, laziness) | ❏ | ❏ |

### My Loving Journal (developing my love-consciousness)
• I felt loved last week when …
• Loving choices I made last week:
• Unloving choices I made last week:
• This week I will love more by …
• This week I will sin less by …

# The Loving Path

*"I have no greater joy than to hear that my children walk in truth." – 3 John 4*

L ife is a journey, and each day presents a new set of challenges on the road to Christlikeness. When met by loving choices, those opportunities bring joy and blessing; when met by unloving choices, they produce sadness and pain. Chapter seven will reveal how sanctification helps Christians make better choices and move to higher expressions of love. Chapter eight will explain how temptation shows one's progress on the pathway of love. Sanctification matures love; temptation measures love. Together they move us further along toward our goal of loving like Jesus.

# Chapter 7

# *Love Matured:*
# Sanctification

*"There is no justification without sanctification, no forgiveness without renewal of life, no real faith from which the fruits of new obedience do not grow." – Martin Luther*

---

When a person becomes a Christian, the work of God is just beginning. The goal is not merely to secure forgiveness, but to transform saved people into the image of God's Son. Yet in both cases, sin is not content to ride quietly into the sunset. Satan will do everything in his power to resist the removal of sin and retake lost ground.

It is no wonder, therefore, that the Bible depicts the Christian life as a holy war that must be waged incessantly. Many question why the sanctification process is so hard and long. The reason is because sin is so deeply rooted in human hearts both individually (our character) and collectively (our culture). It is also because Satan works doggedly to distract Christians from the pursuit of holiness.

## *Sanctification Is a Process*

The struggle against sin is lifelong. In Hebrews 10:10, the writer used the perfect tense to describe sanctification as a completed work: "By that will we have been sanctified through the offering of the body of Jesus Christ once for all." Yet the same writer used the present tense to illustrate the ongoing nature of sanctification: "For by one offering

He has perfected forever those who are being sanctified" (v. 14). The immediate break with sin occurs in conversion, but the commitment to honor that break never ceases. Every day, Christians must renew their love for God and resist the temptations that put their love to the test.

There are three distinct ways to view the work of sanctification.

• *A Position.* When a person becomes a child of God, he experiences a change of status or relationship. The saved person is now part of God's family, earth's redeemed, Christ's body and bride.

• *A Process.* The heart is changed, and the will is committed to honoring the heart's intent.

• *A Product.* A renewed heart results in a reformed life. The inner nature produces a consecrated character and godly conduct.

The word "sanctification" means to separate or set apart. It is a spiritual and behavioral declaration of devotion to God. Sanctification has clear ethical and moral dimensions: it is the practical outworking of a redirected heart. Before laying the foundation of the world, God determined that His people should "be holy and without blame before Him in love" (Ephesians 1:4). In short, sanctification is the process of growing more in love with that which is truly worthy of love.

## The Responsibility of Sanctification

• *Divine Action.* In its primary sense, sanctification is the work of God. Paul prayed, "Now may the God of peace Himself sanctify you completely" (1 Thessalonians 5:23). In addition to the Father's work, the Son and Spirit also play crucial roles in making humans holy. The fundamental ground of sanctification is the atoning death of Jesus (Ephesians 5:25-26; Hebrews 2:11). The opening of the Corinthian letter states, "To the church of God which is at Corinth, to those who are sanctified in Christ Jesus" (1 Corinthians 1:2).

Yet the work of the Spirit is also integral to the sanctification process. Paul attributed the remarkable makeover of the Corinthians to the influence of this third member of the Godhead. After describing the sinfulness of their former lives, he rejoiced, "And such were some of you. But you were washed, but you were sanctified, but you were justified in the name of the Lord Jesus and by the Spirit of our God" (6:11). The Spirit helps Christians match their thoughts, words and deeds with their new spiritual standing. He aids them in making their lives a reflection of their new relationship to Christ. To live that connection to the fullest, to make it real in experience – that is the work of the Spirit (Ephesians 3:16).

• *Human Action.* To this point, the emphasis has been on the Godhead's role in sanctification. Still, there is a secondary sense in which consecration is also the Christian's responsibility. Judgment would not be possible if sanctification depended solely on God's activity. God has provided people with the opportunity, incentive and assistance they need to live holy lives; yet a proper response is required for believers to avail themselves of these blessings. Sanctification, therefore, is a product of holy initiative.

Holiness entails a command to be obeyed and not merely a gift to be received. The Hebrews writer emphasized this connection when he declared, "Pursue peace with all people, and holiness, without which no one will see the Lord" (Hebrews 12:14). Although Peter gloried in the work of the Father, Son and Spirit (1 Peter 1:1-2), he also understood the need for human action and exhorted,

> Therefore gird up the loins of your mind, be sober, and rest your hope fully upon the grace that is to be brought to you at the revelation of Jesus Christ; as obedient children, not conforming yourselves to the former lusts, as in your ignorance; but as He who called you is holy, you also be holy in all your conduct, because it is written, "Be holy, for I am holy" (1 Peter 1:13-16).

Hope rests squarely on grace, but pursuing holiness is essential rather than optional. It is not meritorious; it is indispensable for those who long to see the Lord.

## The Resources of Sanctification

• *Sanctified by Truth.* The pursuit of holiness is not a blind undertaking. The Lord has provided exactly what is needed to make this endeavor successful. Private prayer, public worship and fellowship with other Christians are among the resources He has given us to accomplish this end. Yet, the most fundamental asset in living a sanctified life is God's holy Word. Before leaving the upper room to face His betrayer,

Jesus prayed to the Father for the protection of His disciples. In that critical moment, Jesus implored, "Sanctify them by Your truth, Your word is truth" (John 17:17). Sanctification can only be accomplished through consistent contact with God's revealed will.

When Paul got the opportunity to address leaders in the church, he repeatedly pointed them to the power of Scripture to strengthen and sustain believers. In his meeting with the Ephesian elders at Miletus, he warned them of men who would arise from their own ranks speaking perverse things. How could faithful shepherds prepare for the hour of crisis when gross distortions of truth would be the order of the day? Paul knew just what was needed: "So now, brethren, I commend you to God and to the word of His grace, which is able to build you up and give you an inheritance among all those who are sanctified" (Acts 20:32). In the face of false teaching, nothing can sanctify like God's Word.

• *Sanctified by Faith.* Paul understood that faith in Christ was the key to sanctification (26:18). However, he also knew that the source of faith was divine revelation (Romans 10:17). Spiritual life does not spontaneously generate any more than physical life. Life-containing seed is required. Peter explained,

> Since you have purified your souls in obeying the truth through the Spirit in sincere love of the brethren, love one another fervently with a pure heart, having been born again, not of corruptible seed but incorruptible, through the word of God which lives and abides forever. … Now this is the word which by the gospel was preached to you (1 Peter 1:22-25).

Sanctification is the development of a purer, more fervent love for others through the power of God's Word. It is the end result of believing and obeying what the Spirit has revealed in the gospel regarding authentic expressions of love.

## The Results of Sanctification
Mere exposure to Scripture cannot produce a sanctified life. The Word must sink deep into a saint's heart to have its full effect (Colossians 3:16; James 1:21). Christians must meditate upon God's Word until it permeates their thinking and produces a higher state of consciousness.

When awareness of God's will is combined with awareness of human need, good things begin to happen. Holiness, therefore, is the result of living a more thoughtful life.

Rote memorization of biblical texts can no more provide assurance of spiritual transformation than pretentious prayers, feigned fasting or ostentatious offerings. Religious acts divorced from their intended purpose are nothing but empty rituals (Matthew 6:1-18; 1 Corinthians 13:1-3). God's goal for His people – and the aim underlying every command in Scripture – is to create a community of believers who love others with the heart of Jesus.

The problem is that many churches approach this God-appointed task with one of two mistaken mindsets. Some ignore rigorous study and application of God's Word because they equate love with sentiment. They are more likely to be concerned with principles than particulars. They play fast and loose with God's Word. These congregations are weak and anemic because their faith lacks the sacred structure and spiritual sustenance to maintain a vigorous, healthy love.

Others scrupulously investigate God's Word but lose sight of its overarching purpose. The result can be either cold institutionalism or cruel intimidation. They are traditionalists and terrorists, religious bureaucrats and bullies. In contrast, God's desire for His church is to bear the image of His Son by bearing the burdens of others.

## *Sanctification and Balance*

Balance is the basis of serious sanctification. Proper regard must be given to both positive and negative exhortations in the Bible. Respect must be shown for God's promises as well as His commands. Attention should be paid to large themes and specific instructions.

For some Christians, however, church services are a place to be brutalized on a weekly basis. A preacher with a loud voice and a low self-esteem berates the congregation for failing to measure up to his neurotic standards. In the background, domineering elders pat the preacher on the back for "telling it like it is," and the sickness continues from week to week and generation to generation.

Are there things that must be preached against? Absolutely! But the narrowness and negativity that prevails in many churches is flatly unchristian and more likely to produce con artists and hypochondriacs than mature saints. Doctors and psychologists are called in to apply their secular remedies in treating the emotional sickness of anxiety-ridden souls. Preachers would do well to remember the first obligation of those committed to the healing arts – "Do no harm!"

• *Don't Settle for Guilt.* Some churches are like garden plots where the husbandman spends all his time weeding but never planting. The absence of weeds does not make a garden. The earth must be tilled, seeds must be set, flowers must be watered, and plants must be fertilized. Similarly, souls need to be supported and not just scolded. They must be challenged and not merely criticized. That is why discerning Christians search for growth-oriented congregations with whom they can work and worship (growth meaning spiritual maturity, not secular marketing). The health of their souls and the well-being of their families depend on it.

This balanced approach to Christianity can be seen in Paul's charge to the church in Rome: "For just as you presented your members as slaves of uncleanliness, and of lawlessness leading to more lawlessness, so now present your members as slaves of righteousness for holiness" (Romans 6:19). This formula is repeated in nearly all of Paul's writings. Although he warned the Galatians to abstain from works of the flesh, he concluded by urging them to develop the fruit of the Spirit (Galatians 5:16-26). To the Ephesians and Colossians he advocated putting off the old man in order to put on the new man (Ephesians 4:17-24; Colossians 3:1-17).

From God's perspective, half a life is no life at all. The reason for displacing the bad stuff (sin) is to make room for the good stuff (love). Where does the Bible say that Christians are merely to endure trials and temptations and eke out a timid existence on the earth? Where is the book, chapter and verse that says Christians should hunker down and hang on by the fingernails of their faith until Jesus returns? To paraphrase Philippians 2:15, Paul said saints should shine like pulsating supernovas in a pitch-black night sky. Christians are created by God to stand up and stand out. They are made for spiritual success and significance.

• *Get in the Game.* Victory is God's game. Stopping short of a full and fruitful life is like pitching a shutout without scoring a single run. It is like riding the bench but taking pride in having no errors. Similarly, Christians who take satisfaction in shunning immorality while neglecting their growth and burying their talents have a mistaken view of the Christian life. Sanctification is about fruitful action, not faultless inaction.

Living a negative Christian life is like arriving safely at Disney World but never getting out of the car. Driving defensively is good, but God does not want His children to spend their days in the parking lot of life. He invites us inside to enjoy abundant life. He offers us love and joy in "good measure, pressed down, shaken together, and running over" (Luke 6:38). If a person is not experiencing goodness and mercy on a daily basis, it is not because it is unavailable (Psalm 23:6); it is because he opted for something less. No believer should settle for a guilt-based life when he can choose a growth-based life.

## The Flow of Sanctification

Sanctification is progressive transformation into the image of Christ. This sacred goal requires two things: diminishing love for sin and growing love for the Savior. It is movement from obsession with self to wholehearted dedication to God. When Jesus set Himself apart to fulfill His role as Messiah, it involved more than not doing bad things (John 17:19). Jesus' sacrifice at Calvary demonstrated the entirety of His devotion to God and love for lost men. His dedication was in whole, not in part (10:36). He gave everything He had from the last drop of His blood to the final heave of His chest. No one could love more or better.

Sanctification is the maturing of love. It occurs when Christians turn their hearts from the love and practice of sin to the love and service of God. That love is evidenced in a life of holiness and fruitfulness. It is demonstrated in compassion and kindness. It involves not only refraining from specific acts of sin but also rehabilitating the corrupt source from which those acts emerge. It is a multi-dimensional, soul-stretching experience of the most intense kind.

## Lapses of Love

Jesus' words to an adulterous woman provide special encouragement for those engaged in the ongoing battle against sin (John 8). In forgiving her, He reminded all who struggle with self-hatred or self-doubt that a new and better life really is possible. In telling her to sin no more, He revealed that transformation occurs whenever we look beyond sin's allure to better options that honor Him and improve our lives. Sanctification is about choices – spiritually sound and relationally healthy choices. In essence, it is choosing to love.

But what happens when there are lapses in love in our lives? Like the adulterous woman, Christians are students of spiritual growth with a God-given capacity to learn from their mistakes. Sanctification, therefore, is more about auditing failure than the absence of failure. It is about developing spiritual integrity rather than maintaining delusions of infallibility. Sanctification is the settled determination to love God more and to love more like God.

## Questions

1. Name three distinct ways to describe the work of sanctification.

2. What does the word "sanctification" mean?

3. Sanctification involves the maturing of what?

4. Holiness entails a gift to be received and what else?

5. What is our most fundamental asset for living a sanctified life?

6. Holiness is the result of living what kind of life?

7. Holiness involves the awareness of what two things?

8. What is the result of serious sanctification?

9. Wise Christians should seek what kind of church?

10. What future event proves that sanctification involves a choice?

## Discussion Questions

1. What does it mean to say that sanctification is the maturing of love?

2. What does a growth-oriented church look and feel like?

3. Why is it wrong to equate sanctification with sinlessness?

# Love Quest Survey
## Pursuing a God-Shaped Heart

**Love More**      **(Rate your progress this week)**

My love skills (behaviors that make me MORE loving)    Better – Worse
1. Honesty (realistic, truthful, self-aware)    ❏   ❏
2. Empathy (thoughtful, compassionate, kind, forgiving)    ❏   ❏
3. Responsibility (accountable, reliable, disciplined)    ❏   ❏

My love opportunities – Mark 12:30-31
• God (loving enthusiastically – without reservation)    Better – Worse
1. With all my heart (warm, affectionate love)    ❏   ❏
2. With all my mind (intelligent, informed love)    ❏   ❏
3. With all my strength (energetic, devoted love)    ❏   ❏
4. With all my soul (integrated, holistic love)    ❏   ❏
• Others (loving empathetically – doing good, not harm)    Better – Worse

| | Better | Worse | | Better | Worse |
|---|---|---|---|---|---|
| 1. My mate | ❏ | ❏ | 5. My child | ❏ | ❏ |
| 2. My best friend | ❏ | ❏ | 6. My boss | ❏ | ❏ |
| 3. My co-worker | ❏ | ❏ | 7. My neighbor | ❏ | ❏ |
| 4. My enemy | ❏ | ❏ | 8. My encounters with strangers | ❏ | ❏ |

• Self (loving effectively – bringing out my best self)    Better – Worse
1. My body (caring for my physical needs and health)    ❏   ❏
2. My heart (caring for my emotional needs and self-esteem)    ❏   ❏
3. My mind (caring for my intellectual needs and growth)    ❏   ❏
4. My soul (caring for my spiritual needs and destiny)    ❏   ❏

**Sin Less**      **(Rate your progress this week)**

• My sin snares (behaviors that make me LESS loving)    Better – Worse
1. Irrationality (unrealistic, unaware, untruthful)    ❏   ❏
2. Fabricating (exaggerating, demonizing, romanticizing)    ❏   ❏
3. Insensitivity (uncaring, unkind, unmindful)    ❏   ❏
4. Irresponsibility (undisciplined, unreliable, unaccountable)    ❏   ❏
• My sin challenges (ways I hurt the people I profess to love)   Better – Worse
1. Tongue (gossiping, criticizing, blaming, lying)    ❏   ❏
2. Temper (anger, negativity, intimidation)    ❏   ❏
3. Temptations (lust, pride, selfishness, laziness)    ❏   ❏

## My Loving Journal (developing my love-consciousness)
• I felt loved last week when …
• Loving choices I made last week:
• Unloving choices I made last week:
• This week I will love more by …
• This week I will sin less by …

# Chapter 8

# *Love Tested:*
# Temptation

> "We usually know what we can do, but temptation
> shows us who we are." – Thomas á Kempis

E veryone loves to receive gifts. The word "gift" conjures up pleasant images of a favorite holiday, a sweet 16 party, a high-school graduation, a baby shower, a surprise housewarming, or a romantic candlelit anniversary. Yet some of life's most precious gifts do not come wrapped in brightly colored packages. Not all gifts thrill the heart when they are given and received.

## *Celebrate Temptation*

Although it is seldom welcomed at the time it is bestowed, parental discipline is a precious gift. Proverbs says, "My son, hear the instruction of your father, and do not forsake the law of your mother; for they will be a graceful ornament on your head, and chains about your neck" (1:8-9). In retrospect, mature adults look back on the firmness of household rules with gratitude for the love required to instill those family values (Hebrews 12:11).

Honest counsel is another priceless offering that is often unappreciated (Galatians 4:16). Proverbs explains, "Faithful are the wounds of a friend, but the kisses of an enemy are deceitful" (27:6). Pretend friends specialize in telling others what they want to hear, but true friends are committed to bringing out the best in their companions, although their words may cause twinges of pain. These examples show that life's best gifts are sometimes unusual and unwanted, yet the wise will recognize them for their incomparable worth. Such is the gift of temptation.

James encouraged Christians to celebrate the assorted challenges and calamities that make up life: "My brethren, count it all joy when you fall into various trials" (James 1:2). How can that be? Is it really possible to rejoice in times that are taxing or even tragic? It is possible when they are viewed from a soul perspective. The gift of temptation is not like a new bike or a pony or a diamond ring, but those who are wise prize it far above every worldly possession. In this lesson, we will learn why this is so.

## *The Gift of Self-Awareness*

• *The Spotlight.* The first reason temptation is valuable is because it makes people aware of what is going on inside them. They may have missed the gradual upsurge of their sinful desires. They may have grown careless and let down their guard for a time. James writes, "But each one is tempted when he is drawn away by his own desires and enticed. Then, when desire has conceived, it gives birth to sin; and sin, when it is full-grown, brings forth death. Do not be deceived, my beloved brethren" (1:14-16).

The way temptation blesses is by illuminating the sinful thoughts and desires that have made their home in the heart. It allows people to see what is inside before it gets outside. Temptation is a spiritual spotlight. It has no authority or control over people, but it does reveal what they are contemplating. Becoming aware of desires that diminish spiritual life enables Christians to consider better alternatives.

• *The Biopsy.* Temptation is the spiritual equivalent of a biopsy. It allows people to see the content of their hearts. A biopsy reveals the health or sickness of the body; temptation reveals the health or sickness of the soul. When the body is not well, a biopsy allows the doctor to identify the illness so it may be treated. If the spirit is not well, temptation pinpoints the problem so it may be healed. Locating and labeling disease is critical to health management. Knowing and naming destructive desires is vital to heart management.

Evil not only resides *outside* but also *inside* a Christian. Those who pray for God to deliver them from evil must recognize that the evils from which they most need to be delivered are the sinful attitudes that grip their own hearts. That is why temptation is a gift of sorts: it shows people where they are weak so they don't have to live through the experience of actually committing the harmful act. By reflecting upon temptation rather than merely reacting to it, Christians gain a strategic advantage in their fight against sin.

• *The Time Machine.* Paul said that temptation is always accompanied by a way of escape (1 Corinthians 10:13). The way of escape often comes through anticipating the consequences of sinful acts. The mind is like a time machine that allows Christians to travel into the possibilities of the future to see and feel things in advance. It is possible to foresee that the pleasurable feelings one experiences before sin are almost certain to be replaced by terrible feelings afterward. Temptation is the brightly colored invitation; guilt is the spiritual hangover after the party has ended. Temptation is foresight; guilt is hindsight. Each has the power to awaken the soul, but prevention is always preferable to cure.

Although Satan intends temptation to do harm, God is determined to use it for good. The devil uses it to entangle saints, but God uses it to enlighten them. When temptation reveals a weakening of values or commitment, perceptive saints plug into the power source of heaven to renew their spiritual energy (Ephesians 6:10). Faith is the difference between hardened sinners and humble saints. It is the means by which discerning disciples tap into the strength of the eternal God and attune their minds to love rather than lust.

## *The Gift of Spiritual Growth*

The question is not whether one will experience temptation, but what one will do when it arrives. Alertness is the first step in dealing with spiritual testing, but it is not the only concern. The second step is choosing the right response. Temptation confronts Christians with a choice and requires that they stretch themselves to become better and holier. The Spirit of God nudges saints in the direction of fulfilling their love potential. Change and growth come in direct proportion to the responsible and caring choices one makes. When loving choices are endorsed by the whole heart, transformation occurs.

James declared that God is the giver of every good and perfect gift (James 1:17). One of those gifts is free will. Free will implies the possession of three special skills:

• The ability to recall the results of past choices
• The ability to predict the consequences of future choices
• The ability to act by making present choices

These abilities explain what it means to be created in the image of God because reflecting, projecting and selecting are essential components of loving as God does.

Unloving choices are the essence of sin. Inconsiderate people do not think deeply and are more likely to behave foolishly and selfishly. Lack of love creates the emotional equivalent of blind spots. A blind spot is the area in a driver's field of vision that is not reflected in his mirrors. Similarly, when a person lacks empathy, he is unable to observe the impact of his words and actions on friends, family members and fellow workers. Insensitivity and ingratitude cause him to wreak havoc in others' lives. Worst of all, he is oblivious to the relational carnage left in his wake. The moment a person becomes self-aware is a vital turning point in life. Until this occurs, it is impossible to escape self-defeating patterns of sin.

Christ died not only to redeem mankind from sin but also to remove feelings of hopelessness that keep people from exercising control over their lives. Although one may feel helpless, that bondage is an illusion. To embrace Christ is to embrace choice. Providing the ability to see constructive choices is a vital part of the gospel's power to save. Temptation is neither mightier than Christ nor stronger than the Holy Spirit. Additionally, is it not greater than the person a Spirit-filled, Christ-led man or woman wants to become. Power in the face of temptation is another of God's precious gifts (2 Timothy 1:7).

## *The Gift of Glorifying God*

It is an honor to be asked to perform for a presidential inauguration. The artistic offerings of gifted men and women add dignity and splendor to the occasion; yet how much grander it is to live with the awareness that every day is lived in the presence of the King of kings. He is our audience, and for His pleasure we have been created (Ephesians 2:10). When we triumph over temptation through His power and strength, we glorify His name and delight His heavenly courtiers. Every word of commendation for a life well lived is a tribute to the One who makes such a life possible (Matthew 5:16).

God is glorified whenever His children imitate His example and obey His will. He is magnified by happy homes and true friends. He is exalted by honest CEOs, caring supervisors and industrious employees. Every choice one makes throughout life has the power to bless or burden. Every decision brings honor and happiness or shame and sorrow to others. That is why temptation is a gift of God. It presents a choice, and every choice creates a consequence. Those who choose well have the opportunity to please God and improve the world.

## *Fashion Your Future*

Choice is God's means for enabling people to fashion their own futures. Experience is nothing more than the accumulation of past choices. Character and circumstance, therefore, are the fruits of choice. The day one understands this connection between choice and experience is one of life's greatest moments. It allows farmers to pick the crop they will harvest by carefully selecting the seed they will sow. It allows sailors to reach a desired destination by consulting a map and handling the wheel that guides the rudder. It allows Christians to grow in holiness and steer a course toward heaven.

Of all earth's inhabitants, Christians are in the best position to make the healthiest possible choices. That is because every imaginable resource is available to assist them. The Bible is their map, and the conscience is their compass to keep them on course. The church will correct and encourage Christians, and worship and prayer will sustain them. Faith will influence the full range of their choices from career path and marriage partner to daily habits and dominant attitudes. Yet the most important choice is the purpose for which one lives. Those who make it their mission to love more and better will know the highest joy that is possible this side of heaven.

# Gift Tags

On Dec. 25 each year, multitudes of children wait expectantly for their names to be called as their parents read the tags on gifts taken from beneath the tree. Beneath the tree of Calvary, there is a gift waiting to be opened. The tag says it is from your Father. It is an unspeakable gift that steals the breath of those who hear its contents whispered. It is more precious than silver and gold or anything money can buy. On the tag, written in red, is your name.

Forgiveness is the greatest gift of all because it is the ultimate expression of love. Those who receive this gift are encouraged to share it with others. There is no need to hide it or hoard it because the supply is renewable and inexhaustible.

The power to change your destiny rests in your own hands. Memory, imagination and volition combine to create the possibility of choice, and every choice combines to bring a better future into existence. Even the smallest choice brings the possibility of a more loving future in reach. Temptation is one such choice. It asks, "What do you love?" Remember what past decisions have created in your life and begin selecting those options that maximize your love potential today.

## Questions

1. What is like a graceful ornament on the head?

2. Whose wounds are faithful?

3. Whose kisses are deceitful?

4. What did James say should be counted as joy?

5. What is the spiritual equivalent of a biopsy?

6. What always accompanies temptation?

7. What stands between impulse and action?

8. What is the ultimate expression of love?

9. What three things combine to make choice possible?

10. What does temptation ask?

## Discussion Questions

1. What is the importance of memory in living a more loving life?

2. What is the value of imagination in living a more loving life?

3. How is temptation a gift?

# Love Quest Survey
## Pursuing a God-Shaped Heart

## Love More            (Rate your progress this week)

My love skills (behaviors that make me MORE loving)      Better – Worse
1. Honesty (realistic, truthful, self-aware)                    ❏      ❏
2. Empathy (thoughtful, compassionate, kind, forgiving)         ❏      ❏
3. Responsibility (accountable, reliable, disciplined)          ❏      ❏

My love opportunities – Mark 12:30-31
• God (loving enthusiastically – without reservation)      Better – Worse
1. With all my heart (warm, affectionate love)                  ❏      ❏
2. With all my mind (intelligent, informed love)                ❏      ❏
3. With all my strength (energetic, devoted love)               ❏      ❏
4. With all my soul (integrated, holistic love)                 ❏      ❏
• Others (loving empathetically – doing good, not harm)    Better – Worse

| | | | | Better | Worse |
|---|---|---|---|---|---|
| 1. My mate | ❏ | ❏ | 5. My child | ❏ | ❏ |
| 2. My best friend | ❏ | ❏ | 6. My boss | ❏ | ❏ |
| 3. My co-worker | ❏ | ❏ | 7. My neighbor | ❏ | ❏ |
| 4. My enemy | ❏ | ❏ | 8. My encounters with strangers | ❏ | ❏ |

• Self (loving effectively – bringing out my best self)    Better – Worse
1. My body (caring for my physical needs and health)            ❏      ❏
2. My heart (caring for my emotional needs and self-esteem)  ❏      ❏
3. My mind (caring for my intellectual needs and growth)        ❏      ❏
4. My soul (caring for my spiritual needs and destiny)          ❏      ❏

## Sin Less             (Rate your progress this week)
• My sin snares (behaviors that make me LESS loving)      Better – Worse
1. Irrationality (unrealistic, unaware, untruthful)             ❏      ❏
2. Fabricating (exaggerating, demonizing, romanticizing)        ❏      ❏
3. Insensitivity (uncaring, unkind, unmindful)                  ❏      ❏
4. Irresponsibility (undisciplined, unreliable, unaccountable) ❏   ❏
• My sin challenges (ways I hurt the people I profess to love) Better – Worse
1. Tongue (gossiping, criticizing, blaming, lying)              ❏      ❏
2. Temper (anger, negativity, intimidation)                     ❏      ❏
3. Temptations (lust, pride, selfishness, laziness)             ❏      ❏

## My Loving Journal (developing my love-consciousness)
• I felt loved last week when …
• Loving choices I made last week:
• Unloving choices I made last week:
• This week I will love more by …
• This week I will sin less by …

# The Loving Church

*"If we love one another, God abides in us, and His love has been perfected in us." – 1 John 4:12*

C hristians are soul mates en route to their spiritual homeland. Of all the dangers these pilgrims face, perhaps the greatest is the temptation to lower their sights and settle for a lesser life. Paul described Christianity as an upward calling that elevates saved people to new heights of holiness and joy. The goal of the journey is to glorify God by fulfilling one's love potential. In chapter nine, we will see how fellowship in the church sustains growth in love as saints travel homeward to heaven. In chapter 10, we will learn how caring brethren recover those who grow weary along the way. And in chapter 11, we will discover how Christians recruit followers to Christ and the love-based life. In churches of Christ, love is shared in fellowship, fulfilled in bearing burdens, and multiplied in evangelism. Therefore, the secret to a more loving life is a deeper connection with the loving church.

*Chapter 9*

# *Love Shared:*
# Fellowship

*"I define 'love' thus: The will to extend one's self for
the purpose of nurturing one's own or another's
spiritual growth." – M. Scott Peck*

W hy does the church exist? Why doesn't God simply remove saints
from earth the very instant they are saved? It is because they have
a special mission in this world. They are people with a purpose. The purpose of Christ's church is to help people overcome sin and grow in love.

## *Foundations of Fellowship: The Cross*

The church of Christ is a creation of the cross of Christ. Without Jesus'
death there would be no community and no possibility of unity. Men and
women form many useful social organizations, but only God could dream,
design and deliver a spiritual association perfectly suited to address the
needs of the human soul. The word "association" is preferable to "or-
ganization" or "institution" because it stresses the relational aspects of
*ecclesia*. The church is not only the called out, but also the called together. It is association on a deeper level and with a higher aim.

Divine intervention was necessary to form this fellowship because
sin blocked mankind's path to partnership with God and others. Peace
is possible because Jesus removed the sin barrier at Calvary. His sacrificial love conquered every obstacle that stood in the way of reconciliation and a return to meaningful relationship. What He gave His

church, the members now extend to others. Paul exhorted, "Therefore receive one another, just as Christ also received us, to the glory of God" (Romans 15:7). This means that salvation is both liberation and education. Christians who have tasted God's mercy carry the message of selfless love to a world steeped in sin (non-love) and death (alienation). Passion for evangelism is rooted in our experience of forgiveness.

• *The Preciousness of Fellowship.* Nothing is more precious than time spent with family. Holidays, reunions and birthdays are special occasions that provide joyous memories to be cherished forever. Yet of all God's gifts to His church, fellowship with spiritual family members is the one Christians are most prone to take for granted. Rather than enjoying association with other saints, they are robbed of this pleasure because of idealistic notions about what fellowship looks like. They mistake the church on earth for the kingdom in heaven. The sinless fellowship to be enjoyed in eternity will not be realized on earth. Conversion should bring saints nearer to Christ's image and provide a glimpse of what is to come, but the church is not heaven. The church is a family of heaven-bound souls brought together precisely because they are spiritually immature and in need of assistance in their growth. The church is not God's reward; it is His refinery. Processing plants can be grimy places, though their goal is to produce a pure product. Similarly, churches can be messy, though their goal is to equip saints for ministry and prepare souls for heaven.

Idealism about Christian fellowship is the devil's device. By promoting romantic ideas about the church, Satan hopes to disillusion disciples when they meet head on with relational realities. When unreasonable expectations are not met, they may fall away or search for a new congregation the way a self-indulgent person puts away a mate to look for a "perfect partner." For most people, fellowship is about having others satisfy *their* needs. In contrast, the Bible says Christians should "consider one another" when they come together (Hebrews 10:24). Sporadic attendance patterns are a good indication that a person is thinking of self rather than others. In fellowship, just as in stewardship, it is more blessed to give than to receive.

• *The Preservation of Fellowship.* Just when human love runs low, a resurgence of Christ's love sustains fellowship among brethren. Spiritual love is not about satisfying my desire but fulfilling another's need. Where humans rebuff, the church embraces, and where humans indulge, the church disciplines. The difference is that Christians are motivated by true love for others, whereas the world is motivated by self-love that masquerades as charity. Apart from Christ, love is an imposter, wicked at worst and impure at best.

All families are dysfunctional to some extent, and God's family is no different. Instead of being disillusioned by imperfection in the church, God would have it motivate believers to grow in love. Understanding that people of faith are not without flaws prepares brethren to deal more sympathetically with incidents of sin. Righteous indignation and moral outrage have their place, but compassion for those who struggle with sin is more helpful and appropriate in most cases. Satan is the accuser and divider; saints are the exhorters and unifiers. Each church and each Christian must choose between these identities, and the difference is astounding.

## *Foundations of Fellowship: The Word*

The church is first and foremost a creation of the cross, but it is also a faith community. Fellowship is founded on faith that comes by hearing the Word of God (Romans 10:17). Because the Bible is true, it has the power to enlighten minds, brighten lives and unite hearts. John described the role of the Word in creating community when he wrote, "If we say that we have fellowship with Him, and walk in darkness, we lie and do not practice the truth. But if we walk in the light as He is in the light, we have fellowship with one another, and the blood of Jesus Christ His Son cleanses us from all sin" (1 John 1:6-7). Light is a symbol of divine truth and the holy life it makes possible (Psalm 119:105; Matthew 5:14-16). The church is "the pillar and ground of truth" (1 Timothy 3:15); therefore, Christians live and tell the truth. They exemplify and explain what it really means to love.

• *John 1:1.* What brings Christians together and sustains their relationships with one another is the incarnate Word and His written Word. John wrote, "In the beginning was the Word, and the Word was with God, and the Word was God" (John 1:1). A word is used to express one's mind; therefore, Christ's incarnation was a revelation of the heart and mind of God. Because God is love (1 John 4:8), Jesus provides the fullest and clearest knowledge of what love is and how it works.

To say that Jesus was "the Word" indicates that He was the personification and embodiment of truth about God and His love. But now that Jesus has ascended to heaven, how can Christians avail themselves of this truth? Because the Bible provides an inspired record of Jesus' life and teaching, it is the Word of God communicated through conventional symbols. Because Jesus is light, it is light. Because Jesus is truth, it is truth. Therefore, fellowship is an outgrowth of knowing Jesus through inspired revelation.

• *Colossians 3:14-17*. Life in the church is lived under the authority of the Word, and that is why Christians need each other to be men and women of the Word. In Colossians 3:14-17, Paul urged,

> But above all these things put on love, which is the bond of perfection. And let the peace of God rule in your hearts, to which also you were called in one body; and be thankful. Let the word of Christ dwell in you richly in all wisdom, teaching and admonishing one another in psalms and hymns and spiritual songs, singing with grace in your hearts to the Lord. And whatever you do in word or deed, do all in the name of the Lord Jesus, giving thanks to God the Father through Him.

In these verses, Paul sums up the Christian experience under three main ideas:

(1) The goal – love.

(2) The result – peace.

(3) The means – God's Word.

A casual acquaintance with Scripture will not have the effect God intended. Only when it permeates the soul will peace and completeness be possible. Through studying God's Word, Christians learn how to love one another and maintain unity in the body of Christ.

## A Model for Fellowship

The biblical model for Christian fellowship is an outgrowth of four crucial questions.

• *What?* What is God's purpose for calling His people into relationship with one another? The answer is "maturity." His intention is to sanctify them through association with one another.

• *How?* How is God's purpose of spiritual formation accomplished? The answer is "study." Saints are shaped by their encounters with the living Word of God.

• *Who?* Who is God using to instruct and exhort His disciples? The answer is "community." Support for spiritual growth is found in the fellowship of the church.

• *Why?* Why is God determined to mold members of His church into the image of His Son? The answer is "ministry." Christians are transformed to increase their effectiveness as ministers of reconciliation.

The goal of maturing saints for ministry is accomplished through time spent in the Word of God and among His people. The effect of loving instruction and counsel in the church is to provide Christians with a greater sense of reality than one can obtain on his own. Helping a brother become more aware of his true spiritual condition must be followed by providing him with support needed for taking responsible action. One cannot pass to spiritual maturity and effective ministry without first embracing reality and responsibility. The process goes this way:

Study – Community – Reality – Responsibility – Maturity – Ministry

## *Responsibilities of Fellowship*

Fellowship is unquestionably a gift, but it does not come without responsibilities. In order to maintain the unity of the Spirit in the bond of peace, each must do his part to help the community grow in love. Love is promoted whenever Christians meet together to worship God in spirit and truth. They bring their faith to bear in each other's lives in God-ordained ways that produce healthy spiritual growth. In doing this, the body of Christ is better prepared to love and serve a lost world.

The stated purpose of Christian worship is to excite love, which is expressed in doing good to others: "And let us consider one another in order to stir up love and good works, not forsaking the assembling of ourselves together, as is the manner of some, but exhorting one another, and so much the more as you see the Day approaching" (Hebrews 10:24-25). Christians challenge each other to be faithful in coming together because they know that absence reflects a waning of love that will only grow worse without fellowship to rekindle the heart's devotion. God uses singing, praying, preaching, communing and giving to promote love among His people.

## How Worship Promotes Love

• *Singing.* Singing connects Christians to one another by mingling the message of the gospel with the power of music. Music has a way of touching hearts as nothing else can. Yet the critical factor is not the melody or rhyme, but the words sung in the heart. That is why singing can produce immense joy regardless of musical ability. The music of the soul is the rhythm of love that reverberates in a redeemed heart. When souls are centered on the Lord and His teaching, people are brought closer to each other as they are brought closer to Him. This is harmony indeed!

• *Praying.* Praying bonds believers by bringing them jointly into the presence of God to petition and praise Him. The leader is granted permission to direct the attention of worshipers to past blessings, present needs and future promises. Like travelers who have grown closer during their journey together, Christians grow more intimate as they prayerfully visit the missionary in the field, the member in the hospital, and the Maker in His throne room. The most powerful moment in prayer comes when all who are present unite their wills in full agreement by saying, "Amen!"

• *Communing.* The Lord's Supper links believers' lives as they gather around a common table. At ordinary mealtimes, food fills hungry stomachs, but it also unites souls that are starving for fellowship. Those who want to build relationships with others look for opportunities to break bread with them. Eating the Lord's Supper is networking of a spiritual kind. As Jesus seeks to solidify relationships among saints, He calls them together around His table. As they are drawn closer in proximity, they are drawn closer in personality. Fellowship does not produce clones, but it does produce Christlikeness.

• *Preaching.* Preaching fuses hearts by fixing worshipers' minds on the words and works of Christ. The gospel revolutionizes relationships by altering the way people think. Paul understood that the church's unity was rooted in common beliefs that grow out of a collective thought process:

> Now I plead with you, brethren, by the name of our Lord
> Jesus Christ, that you all speak the same thing, and that there
> be no divisions among you, but that you be perfectly joined
> together in the same mind and in the same judgment. For it
> has been declared to me concerning you, my brethren, by
> those of Chloe's household, that there are contentions among
> you (1 Corinthians 1:10-11).

Contentions result from thoughts that are uncaring and unloving. Thinking Christianly is a foundation of fellowship, but fellowship is also a component of thinking Christianly.

• *Giving.* Giving is God's way of reminding Christians about the sacrificial essence of love. It is also a proven means of entwining human hearts. Jesus said, "For where your treasure is, there your heart will be also" (Matthew 6:21). Souls are interwoven by their common interests. That is why fellowship is partnership. Caring about the same things brings hearts closer together, and sharing financially in the work of God cements souls as few things can.

Assembling to worship is only one of God's ways for making the church a more loving community. Although it is essential, it is just part of the responsibility of Christian camaraderie. How saints interact when they come together is the real test of meaningful fellowship. What did God intend to transpire when Christians come in contact? Consider the seven duties of discipleship in the next section and note the increasing intimacy they require.

## Facets of Fellowship

• *Engaging.* The church was made to supply a deeper level of relationship than the world is capable of providing. Most relating that occurs on a daily basis happens on a shallow, impersonal level and cannot touch the soul or fill its genuine needs. Even clubs that draw people together around mutual interests lack the quality of associations in the church. The Society for the Preservation and Encouragement of Barbershop Quartet Singing is not of interest to all people and is not concerned about eternity. The focus of fellowship, therefore, is to engage others at the soul level. The interests that draw Christians together are not amusements or diversions. They are universal, vital and deeply relational concerns. When the church comes together, souls touch in ways that stimulate growth in love. That is why assembly times are so important. When a Christian misses a service, he misses out on God's means for making him more loving. When he forsakes the assembly, therefore, he is less loving than he would have been had he spent time in God's Word with God's people.

• *Edifying.* When Jude wrote a letter to encourage faithful brethren who were battling false teachers, he urged them to build themselves up in the most holy faith (Jude 20). The teaching and preaching of God's Word that occur when Christians come together are for the purpose of fortifying faith. God's Word is powerful any time it is studied, but fellowship with God's people enhances its effects. In community, there is greater opportunity to clarify biblical understanding and modify unchristian behavior. It is God's intention for Christians to be strengthened in love by saturating their hearts with Scripture. Edification is the key to living effectively and loving successfully.

• *Exhorting.* At the moment of conversion, Christians implicitly enter a pact to provide mutual soul-care for one another. They agree to intercede in each other's lives whenever they observe spiritual opportunities or dangers (Hebrews 3:13). Failure to intervene is a failure to love. Although it is common for neglectful saints to label their inaction as compassion, more often than not they are engaging in self-preservation. The feelings they truly want to spare are their own. It can be painful and risky to confront others with the reality of their lives, but Christians must have the courage to be candid when love demands it. They must also be approachable and appreciative when others care enough to admonish them. Spiritual maturity is the ability to hear advice without losing your self-control or your self-esteem.

• *Envisioning.* One of the most positive ways to assist in the spiritual formation of fellow Christians is to provide them with a new self-image to challenge their growth. The angel said to Gideon, "The Lord is with you, you mighty man of valor!" (Judges 6:12). Gideon eventually became one of the greatest judges in Israel, but it all began with the promising words of a hopeful herald. Christians are God's motivational messengers today. It is their job to lift saints above the barrier of their limited expectations. It is not enough to scrutinize others' lives and label the sin from which they are suffering. The church must go beyond analyzing sin's pathology to assess the soul's possibilities. In the fellowship of the redeemed, Christians receive a new vision of the future and their own place in it. When others see good in them, they are more capable of seeing it themselves. Words of promise inspire people to tap into the potential that God placed within their souls.

• *Encouraging.* Once a Christian captures an image of the new person he can become, the arduous journey of transformation has just begun. Where does he get the confidence and emotional energy needed to continue growing? The fellowship of the church provides the support necessary to defeat doubt and discouragement. Paul wrote, "Therefore comfort each other and edify one another, just as you also are doing" (1 Thessalonians 5:11). When a brother in Christ falls short of his expectations, the church comforts. When he feels like giving up, the church edifies. The strategy differs, but the goal remains the same – sustain effort! Inside every person there are competing urges that vie for supremacy. Satan will use every means to strengthen sinful urges, and saints are equally determined to support the teachings of the Spirit. The flesh strives for ascendancy, but the love of Christ and His Church tips the scale in favor of the higher impulses of the soul.

• *Embracing.* Bearing burdens is the business of the church (Galatians 6:2), but it is not possible to embrace the pain and problems of others while remaining physically or emotionally distant. Love is not aloof, yet it is far too common for pews to be filled with smiling, well-dressed saints who merely pretend to have fellowship. God's desire is for Christians to become so real and so close that grace is required to sustain the relationship. Only then can real fellowship and growth take place. Christ's compassion led Him first to earth and then to Calvary. He bore the cross not only to save mankind, but also to show the burden-bearing nature of love. The church is His body doing His work; therefore, when Christians do not forbear, forgive and foster love, they deny Christ and break His supreme law.

• *Extending.* In describing the function of the church, Paul prayed that Christians, "may grow up in all things into Him who is the head – Christ – from whom the whole body, joined and knit together by what every joint supplies, according to the effective working by which every part does its share, causes growth of the body for the edifying of itself in love" (Ephesians 4:15-16). The point is that love causes each member of Christ's body to stretch to fulfill its responsibility to the others. This is the goal of fellowship.

Each of the preceding points contributes in some way to this supreme objective. At first, the apostles had difficulty grasping this concept. Whereas they argued about greatness, Jesus redefined greatness. A great life is one of sacrificial love that finds its highest joy in serving others (Romans 12:16; Philippians 2:1-4). That is why preoccupation and inflexibility are sins just as much as adultery. God is constantly channeling people to His church to be helped and blessed. Loving those who are sent is seldom convenient, but it remains God's challenge to receive them eagerly and serve them energetically.

## The Flawed but Faithful Church

These are just a few of the reasons that the church comes together in fellowship. Unfortunately, many people continue to think of "church" in ways that Jesus never intended. The church is not masonry, bureaucracy or pageantry. It is people passionately in love with God and with those created in His image. Foremost, it is a sacred relationship.

Jesus dreamed of establishing a church that would introduce the healing power of love to a troubled world. That church would also be His means of transforming saints into caring people who could carry out this mission with credibility. The divine design and supporting structure of the church are as perfect as the mind that conceived them. However, the creaturely side of the church is as imperfect as a fallen heart.

The human failings of the church do not discredit Christ's plan; they merely emphasize why the church's work is important and must continue. It is not shocking that sin commonly appears among God's people, but it is astounding that so much love can be found among those not yet fully redeemed. Until Christ returns, the church will always be a work in progress. Love will continue to emerge in surprising ways and at unexpected times, but sin will always be nearby. That means that Christ is not only the hope of a chronically dysfunctional world, but also of a recurrently dysfunctional church that is bathed in His blood and readied to do battle with sin again and again.

## *Questions*

1. What are the two foundations of fellowship?

2. What is a symbol of divine truth that enlightens the mind?

3. What is the bond of perfection?

4. What are the four elements in the biblical model for fellowship?

5. How does Hebrews 10:24-25 say that love is expressed?

6. What is networking of a spiritual kind?

7. What results from uncaring and unloving thoughts?

8. What touches when the church comes together in fellowship?

9. What is the purpose of encouragement?

10. What is required for Christians to maintain close relations?

## *Discussion Questions*

1. Why doesn't God remove people from earth the instant they are saved?

2. How do romantic notions about the church undermine fellowship?

3. Explain why human failings do not discredit Christ's plan for His church.

# Love Quest Survey
## Pursuing a God-Shaped Heart

**Love More**          **(Rate your progress this week)**

My love skills (behaviors that make me MORE loving)     Better – Worse
1. Honesty (realistic, truthful, self-aware)     ❏     ❏
2. Empathy (thoughtful, compassionate, kind, forgiving)     ❏     ❏
3. Responsibility (accountable, reliable, disciplined)     ❏     ❏

My love opportunities – Mark 12:30-31
• God (loving enthusiastically – without reservation)     Better – Worse
1. With all my heart (warm, affectionate love)     ❏     ❏
2. With all my mind (intelligent, informed love)     ❏     ❏
3. With all my strength (energetic, devoted love)     ❏     ❏
4. With all my soul (integrated, holistic love)     ❏     ❏
• Others (loving empathetically – doing good, not harm)     Better – Worse

| | | | | | |
|---|---|---|---|---|---|
| 1. My mate | ❏ | ❏ | 5. My child | ❏ | ❏ |
| 2. My best friend | ❏ | ❏ | 6. My boss | ❏ | ❏ |
| 3. My co-worker | ❏ | ❏ | 7. My neighbor | ❏ | ❏ |
| 4. My enemy | ❏ | ❏ | 8. My encounters with strangers | ❏ | ❏ |

• Self (loving effectively – bringing out my best self)     Better – Worse
1. My body (caring for my physical needs and health)     ❏     ❏
2. My heart (caring for my emotional needs and self-esteem)     ❏     ❏
3. My mind (caring for my intellectual needs and growth)     ❏     ❏
4. My soul (caring for my spiritual needs and destiny)     ❏     ❏

**Sin Less**          **(Rate your progress this week)**

• My sin snares (behaviors that make me LESS loving)     Better – Worse
1. Irrationality (unrealistic, unaware, untruthful)     ❏     ❏
2. Fabricating (exaggerating, demonizing, romanticizing)     ❏     ❏
3. Insensitivity (uncaring, unkind, unmindful)     ❏     ❏
4. Irresponsibility (undisciplined, unreliable, unaccountable)     ❏     ❏
• My sin challenges (ways I hurt the people I profess to love)     Better – Worse
1. Tongue (gossiping, criticizing, blaming, lying)     ❏     ❏
2. Temper (anger, negativity, intimidation)     ❏     ❏
3. Temptations (lust, pride, selfishness, laziness)     ❏     ❏

## My Loving Journal (developing my love-consciousness)
• I felt loved last week when …
• Loving choices I made last week:
• Unloving choices I made last week:
• This week I will love more by …
• This week I will sin less by …

# Chapter 10

# Love Fulfilled:
# Restoration

> *"The cure for all ills and wrongs, the cares, the sorrows and the crimes of humanity, all lie in the one word 'love.' It is the divine vitality that everywhere produces and restores life."*
> *– Lydia Maria Child*

Nowhere is Christianity's magnificence more evident than in the way Christians are to treat human failure. Everyone sins and falls short of God's glory (Romans 3:23), but everyone also misses the mark of his own expectations. Consider the following note I received from a young man in his teens whom I had baptized.

Dear Mr. Johnson,

Thank you for all the help you've been. There was just one thing I was wondering. Since I'm officially in God's family now, I want to know how to change my life. Right now, I'm feeling a bit sad since my life hasn't changed much, if at all. I don't seem to have the "fountain of joy" within me. I think I know why.

Really, I just want to know how to change my life to live like God wants me to. I feel depressed because I just don't seem to be living my life according to God's will. If you have any advice, I'd be glad to hear it. Please respond as soon as possible! Thanks.

What is a person to do ...
• When he feels spiritually stuck?
• When transformation seems to be taking too long?
• When confronted with a gnawing sense of personal failing?

The answer I gave my young friend was twofold. First, we talked about God's plan for producing positive change in life. Although perfection is not possible, significant growth can and should occur over time. The Bible is the world's best source of information on personal development and spiritual growth.

Then we discussed how to handle the surge of emotions he was experiencing. Listen to the words he used: "I'm feeling a bit sad ... I don't seem to have the 'fountain of joy' within me ... I feel depressed." Who has not shared those sentiments at one time or another? I suggested he would find the answers he was looking for in closer fellowship with God's people. The Word provides essential knowledge for growth, but the church provides necessary support for growth. God's family was designed to be a safe environment for tackling tough problems and processing painful feelings in a spiritually healthy way.

• *The Healing Church.* Sometimes shortcomings are private, and Christians try to deal with them on their own. Privacy is not always a good idea because it severely limits the resources available for solving problems. At other times, failures are public, and the church as a group comes into play. Although people typically dread this, it is a positive thing. Just as the human body rushes aid to restore its injured parts, the body of Christ sends healing agents to help its wounded members. The role of the church is to cure and not merely to censure (John 3:17; Luke 6:37). Unfortunately, well-intentioned saints have sometimes been known to worsen problems rather than alleviate them.

Paul understood this danger and addressed it in a letter to the troubled church at Galatia. New Christians were struggling in their walk with God and desperately needed assistance. What was the church's responsibility in this matter? Listen to Paul's instructions:

> Brethren, if a man is overtaken in any trespass, you who are spiritual restore such a one in a spirit of gentleness, considering yourself lest you also be tempted. Bear one another's

burdens, and so fulfill the law of Christ. For if anyone thinks himself to be something, when he is nothing, he deceives himself. But let each one examine his own work, and then he will have rejoicing in himself alone, and not in another. For each one shall bear his own load (Galatians 6:1-5).

## *The Problem*

• *Frame It.* Paul's instruction began with a word that is often overlooked: "Brethren." When confronting a problem, it is always important to frame it correctly. Consider the difficulty that arose between the herdsmen of Abraham and Lot over a shortage of pasture for their livestock. In resolving the issue, Abraham knew it was crucial to remind his nephew of their kinship: "Please let there be no strife between you and me, and between my herdsmen and your herdsmen; for we are brethren" (Genesis 13:8). Abraham made it clear from the start: "This problem is not bigger than our relationship." Without that consideration, a battle might have broken out. Instead, a caring mood was established that allowed them to work out the crisis with civil words rather than civil war.

For Christians, problems should always be considered in the context of their relationship to Christ (2 Thessalonians 3:14-15). All interactions must be guided by consciousness of this spiritual connection. However great the sin, family love should overshadow all that is said and done. If a person has trouble keeping this in mind, it would be better to let someone else undertake the intervention.

Compassion provides the most favorable context for helping others face harmful behaviors such as aggression, addiction or apostasy. Whether the problem is emotional, physical or doctrinal, love is the key to optimizing outcomes. Firmness may be in order, but if the approach is perceived as an attack, progress is unlikely. The relationship creates the atmosphere in which the problem is solved. The stronger the bond, the better the outcome. If the relationship is weak, it will be unable to bear the discomfort of direct communication. If the relationship is sturdy, it is possible to face the problem squarely and do the hard work required to move forward.

• *Name It.* Paul described the sin in Galatians 6 as a "trespass." This terminology is not incidental to the healing process. It helps because it places the responsibility for the trouble right where it belongs: in the lap of the sinner. Regardless of the instigation of the evil one, sin is always a personal choice (James 1:14-16).

The Hebrew word for trespass means to step aside from the proper path (Genesis 31:36). Similarly, the Greek word refers to falling aside (Ephesians 2:1). In both cases, the doer has departed from the correct course of action. A breach of ethical behavior has occurred: the perpetrator has broken away from God's will and violated His Word.

Acknowledging blameworthiness is helpful rather than hurtful. No one likes to admit fault, but it puts a handle on the problem. It acknowledges that no victimization has occurred. It is an admission that the trouble is internal rather than external. This awareness puts people in the driver's seat of life where they can steer a brand new course. Failure to own faults is like ripping the steering wheel from a dashboard and throwing it in the back seat. Disconnecting the steering mechanism from a car results in a loss of control over the vehicle; disconnecting choices from their consequences results in a loss of control over one's life. Dodging responsibility does not make for safe driving or spiritual development.

In general terms, a trespass is a form of unloving behavior. Identifying the specific sin gives one the ability to take appropriate action to correct it. In Galatians 5:19-21, Paul provided a sample list of some of the most common problem behaviors that undermine people's happiness and relationships.

> Now the works of the flesh are evident, which are: adultery, fornication, uncleanliness, lewdness, idolatry, sorcery, hatred, contentions, jealousies, outbursts of wrath, selfish ambitions, dissensions, heresies, envy, murders, drunkenness, revelries, and the like; of which I tell you beforehand, just as I also told you in time past, that those who practice such things will not inherit the kingdom of God.

Seventeen sins are identified by Paul and two major themes emerge from this inventory: immorality and anger. Both problems involve a loss of self-control. The degree of control one displays in life usually

determines the amount of satisfaction one derives from life. That is because successful relationships are a by-product of self-discipline. For
instance, unfaithfulness and unkindness damage marriages and friendships but commitment and courtesy strengthen them. Greater control
equals greater love.

• *Sustain It*. When Paul said some Galatians were "overtaken" in a
trespass, he did not mean that the pressure was more than they could
bear and that they were deprived of choice in the matter. He was not
saying that they were unable to help themselves and that resistance was
futile. The Galatians were not without responsibility. The question was
how to hold them responsible in the most loving way.

To be "overtaken" simply means that a change had occurred in the
ruling principle of their lives. Their spiritual orientation had shifted.
Battles are always raging within believers, and sometimes fleshly urges
get the upper hand. Yet this should be the exception and not the rule.
Disciples cannot allow their default condition to be one of carnality.
The normative state for Christians is to be Spirit-led. The deeds of
the lower nature must be brought under control or, better yet, put to
death (Romans 8:13).

It is important to recognize that a saint's struggle between higher and
lower impulses will never end during this lifetime. Although some sins
will be laid to rest permanently, new challenges will always arise. The
Spirit and flesh continually vie for supremacy, and fluctuations occur
even among people of faith. This changeable condition was clearly evident among the Corinthians to whom Paul wrote the following words:

> And I, brethren, could not speak to you as to spiritual peo-
> ple but as to carnal, as to babes in Christ. I fed you with milk
> and not with solid food; for until now you were not able to
> receive it, and even now you are still not able; for you are
> still carnal. For where there are envy, strife, and divisions
> among you, are you not carnal and behaving like mere men?
> (1 Corinthians 3:1-3).

Paul was urging the Corinthians to pursue growth and greater consistency. Helping Christians sustain spiritual progress is the goal of
leaders in the church. Although worship, Bible study and fellowship

help improve and regulate the Christian life, everyone experiences times when direct intervention by caring brethren is essential. When that time comes, Paul spelled out what should happen next.

## *The Plan*

God's plan for getting struggling saints back on their feet begins with the word "you." Spiritual intervention is not merely the job of elders, preachers, youth ministers and deacons. Caring confrontation is everyone's job! Hebrews 3:13 urges, "But exhort one another daily, while it is called 'Today,' lest any of you be hardened through the deceitfulness of sin." Mutual soul care should be ongoing and spontaneous rather than infrequent and formal.

• *Limitation.* Paul gave one limiting factor regarding those who are suited to undertake this mission of mercy – they must be "spiritual." Those who are guided by the flesh rather than the Spirit are more likely to do harm than good. The effective interventionist will be one who walks by the Spirit (Galatians 5:16, 25). One who lacks the fruit of the Spirit lacks the relational tools and temperament necessary to succeed in the job (vv. 22-24). In contrast, the spiritual man or woman is uniquely prepared and positioned to salvage sin-wrecked souls.

• *Restoration.* The aim of the spiritual man or woman is to restore the one overtaken in a trespass. To restore means to return something to its previous or original condition. This task involves two steps. The first step requires helping a person caught up in self-defeating behavior to stop loving and repeating the counterproductive actions that are ruining his life. The next step is to assist him in a return to the Spirit-led condition he previously enjoyed so he may continue on a path of personal growth and effective ministry.

• *Examination.* The key to restoration is guiding transgressors through a process of self-examination. Because change requires discontent, the interventionist must help them realistically assess the consequences of their selfish choices. If they are honest, they will admit their dissatisfaction with sin's effects in their lives. The spiritual man or woman uses the power of imagination to show transgressors the future so they can envision what they will suffer and sacrifice if they do not repent. Sin is a poor bargain, and the goal is to induce righteous regret. This spiritual awakening is comparable to the experience of a consumer who discovers he has been duped by a cunning salesman. Godly sorrow is the buyer's remorse of a swindled soul (Matthew 16:26).

• *Inspiration.* Spirit-minded people supply the catalyst for lasting, positive change, but they must do more than point out the wrongdoing of others. They must also persuade transgressors of God's willingness to forgive their sins and assist their growth. In other words, to restore right thinking and right living, one must also restore hope. Criticism may highlight the need for change, but it takes encouragement to initiate and sustain it.

• *Invitation.* A spirit of gentleness is vital to the restoration process. Paul selected this kindly characteristic to illustrate the need for qualified people to undertake this important work. It cannot be entered into lightly, nor can just anyone succeed in it. A humble, unpretentious attitude is more likely to reach a backsliding brother than an air of superiority. The first says, "I am like you." The second says, "Why can't you be like me?" One extends a warm invitation, but the other issues a cold demand.

## *The Precaution*

Paul was concerned not only about the transgressor's troubles but also for the restorer who was susceptible to wrongdoing while engaging in the recovery process. Paul advised rescuers to consider themselves lest they also be tempted. Danger is always present when dealing with the sins of others. One such hazard is self-righteousness. Paul exhorted the Corinthians, "Therefore let him who thinks he stands take heed lest he fall" (1 Corinthians 10:12). The overconfidence and arrogance Paul warned against is detectable in the attitude of the Pharisee in Jesus' parable against the perils of pride (Luke 18:9-14). The Pharisee's lack of empathy for the publican's plight was contrary to the gentle spirit that a servant of the Lord should possess. Concerning spiritual leaders, Paul wrote,

> And a servant of the Lord must not quarrel but be gentle to all, able to teach, patient, in humility correcting those who are in opposition, if God perhaps will grant them repentance,

so that they may know the truth, and that they may come to their senses and escape the snare of the devil, having been taken captive by him to do his will (2 Timothy 2:24-26).

A harsh, haughty attitude does little to build strong connections with those whose destructive behaviors have made them their own worst enemies. Because they are held captive by mistaken ideas, the interventionist must provide them with knowledge to free them from their wrong beliefs. However, Paul knew that the manner in which teaching is presented makes a difference. Combining truth with the right technique is critical for recovering wayward Christians. Effective interventionists are caring coaches rather than callous critics.

• *Burden Bearers.* Jesus warned His followers against rushing prematurely to judgment (Matthew 7:1-6). Those who are quick to repudiate and disassociate are more likely to aggravate problems than alleviate them. In most cases, the right method for restoring transgressors is a gentle, burden-bearing approach.

But what is the burden in need of bearing? Is it not the feelings of helplessness and worthlessness produced by guilt? When a person becomes aware of dishonorable deeds, it is not the time to pile on blame. It is time to lift the load. The work of restoration calls for empathy that enables one to suffer with the transgressor and feel his pain. By identifying with him and sympathizing with him, the interventionist gains his trust and the ability to reach him.

• *Law Fulfillers.* By bearing the burdens of others, Christians automatically fulfill the law of Christ (Matthew 22:39). Because Jesus bore their burdens, appreciative saints are eager to do the same for someone else. Harassing the spiritually weak is unthinkable for those who are recipients of grace. Spirit-led men and woman are supporters of besieged believers and stand ready to assist them in their return to righteous living.

Paul's admonition to bear one another's burdens brought him back to his earlier warning against a smug spirit. He added, "For if anyone thinks himself to be something, when he is nothing, he deceives himself" (Galatians 6:3). This counsel was essential to protect interventionists from the dangers of pride. God's helpers need a proper understanding of their own need for mercy if they are to motivate change in others. Ministers of God's grace must operate with an awareness of their own need for grace. Haughtiness is unholy and unhelpful in the work of restoration. No matter how discerning and devout one may be, he is "nothing" if he fails to deal compassionately with the sins of others (1 Corinthians 13:2-3).

• *Truth Testers.* The apostle's next step was to call on each man to examine his own work. The interventionist's "work" is to restore those whose spiritual progress has been halted by sin. To "examine" means to prove or test with the implied intent of getting better (2 Corinthians 8:8). In this context, it refers to probing beneath actions to appraise underlying motives (2 Corinthians 13:5). Are they consistent with the purpose of Christ and the teaching of the Spirit? Do they exemplify love for people or for authority? Spiritual men and women constantly assess the practice of their faith to improve their effectiveness as God's servants.

But how does proving take place? It occurs whenever actions and attitudes are compared with the Word of God. Scripture is the standard because it reveals the life and mind of Christ, which serve as a pattern for believers to follow (1 Peter 2:21). A Christian should ask, "Is my behavior consistent with the spirit of Christ and His standard of love?"

Unfortunately, some are intent on justifying their sins rather than improving their lives. This motivation leads them to assess their shortcomings through comparisons with fellow mortals rather than the flawless Master. The problem is that using the wrong measure inevitably leads to the wrong assessment. Dwelling on the lowest point in another person's life will never excuse my sins. It can inflate my ego, but it cannot enlarge my heart. It can make me feel better, but it will not make me better.

Proper self-estimates result from examining behavior in light of the church's exalted purpose – to love like Christ! On this basis, there is never an occasion for spiritual complacency. Because God reveals the meaning of love and the possibility of love, all praise and honor belong to Him. Through the Bible the meaning of love is illuminated. In the fellowship of the church the power to love is activated. No person can reach his full love potential outside of a relationship with Jesus and His church.

• *Soul Supporters.* Although Christians assist each other in the struggle against sin, final accountability rests with each individual for the life-choices he has made. When brethren fail in their duty to provide spiritual support, it does not justify the sinner's selfishness and irresponsibility. Paul declared, "For each one shall bear his own load" (Galatians 6:5). On judgment day, every human being will account for himself. Others can help along the way, but destiny is one's own doing.

The love of the church is a powerful resource in the fight against sin, yet only the love of Christ is sufficient to save one from sin. There is a vast difference between soul supporters and the soul's Savior, although they seek the same end: a life of love that abounds to the glory of the Father.

Christians play a limited support role in the scheme of redemption, but it would be a terrible mistake to underestimate their value. The loving Christ works through His loving people to redeem the lost. It is their supreme privilege to proclaim the gospel and reclaim the wayward. How joyful to be the face of Jesus to love-starved souls: to be the eyes in which they see the concern of Christ and the voice in which they hear the hope of heaven.

The responsibility of burden bearing is immense, but the rewards are immeasurable. The pain can be intense, but the pleasure of a soul saved is incomparable. To bear another's burden is the loftiest honor and the highest joy one can know on earth. It is what you were created for and something truly worth dying for. It is your calling and your choice.

## Questions

1. What are spiritual people instructed to do with brethren caught in sin?

2. Which fruit of the Spirit does Paul highlight for restoring wayward brethren?

3. What was the qualification Paul gave for anyone attempting to restore others?

4. What must each bear?

5. What should each one examine?

6. In what are Christians said to be overtaken?

7. To frame the problem, what did Paul ask the Galatians to remember?

8. When Christians bear one another's burdens, what do they fulfill?

9. Why are Christians told to consider themselves when dealing with other's sins?

10. One who examines his own work will have rejoicing in whom?

## *Discussion Questions*

1. What impresses you about Christianity's treatment of human failure?

2. How would you answer the young man who was recently baptized?

3. Share a time when someone helped you bear a personal burden.

# Love Quest Survey
## Pursuing a God-Shaped Heart

## Love More       (Rate your progress this week)

My love skills (behaviors that make me MORE loving)    Better – Worse

|  | Better | Worse |
|---|---|---|
| 1. Honesty (realistic, truthful, self-aware) | ❏ | ❏ |
| 2. Empathy (thoughtful, compassionate, kind, forgiving) | ❏ | ❏ |
| 3. Responsibility (accountable, reliable, disciplined) | ❏ | ❏ |

My love opportunities – Mark 12:30-31

• God (loving enthusiastically – without reservation)    Better – Worse

|  | Better | Worse |
|---|---|---|
| 1. With all my heart (warm, affectionate love) | ❏ | ❏ |
| 2. With all my mind (intelligent, informed love) | ❏ | ❏ |
| 3. With all my strength (energetic, devoted love) | ❏ | ❏ |
| 4. With all my soul (integrated, holistic love) | ❏ | ❏ |

• Others (loving empathetically – doing good, not harm)    Better – Worse

| | Better | Worse | | Better | Worse |
|---|---|---|---|---|---|
| 1. My mate | ❏ | ❏ | 5. My child | ❏ | ❏ |
| 2. My best friend | ❏ | ❏ | 6. My boss | ❏ | ❏ |
| 3. My co-worker | ❏ | ❏ | 7. My neighbor | ❏ | ❏ |
| 4. My enemy | ❏ | ❏ | 8. My encounters with strangers | ❏ | ❏ |

• Self (loving effectively – bringing out my best self)    Better – Worse

|  | Better | Worse |
|---|---|---|
| 1. My body (caring for my physical needs and health) | ❏ | ❏ |
| 2. My heart (caring for my emotional needs and self-esteem) | ❏ | ❏ |
| 3. My mind (caring for my intellectual needs and growth) | ❏ | ❏ |
| 4. My soul (caring for my spiritual needs and destiny) | ❏ | ❏ |

## Sin Less       (Rate your progress this week)

• My sin snares (behaviors that make me LESS loving)    Better – Worse

|  | Better | Worse |
|---|---|---|
| 1. Irrationality (unrealistic, unaware, untruthful) | ❏ | ❏ |
| 2. Fabricating (exaggerating, demonizing, romanticizing) | ❏ | ❏ |
| 3. Insensitivity (uncaring, unkind, unmindful) | ❏ | ❏ |
| 4. Irresponsibility (undisciplined, unreliable, unaccountable) | ❏ | ❏ |

• My sin challenges (ways I hurt the people I profess to love) Better – Worse

|  | Better | Worse |
|---|---|---|
| 1. Tongue (gossiping, criticizing, blaming, lying) | ❏ | ❏ |
| 2. Temper (anger, negativity, intimidation) | ❏ | ❏ |
| 3. Temptations (lust, pride, selfishness, laziness) | ❏ | ❏ |

## My Loving Journal (developing my love-consciousness)
• I felt loved last week when …
• Loving choices I made last week:
• Unloving choices I made last week:
• This week I will love more by …
• This week I will sin less by …

# Chapter 11

# Love Multiplied:
# Evangelism

*"You will find as you look back upon your life that the moments when you have truly lived are the moments when you have done things in the spirit of love."* – Henry Drummond

It is often said that the mission of the church is to evangelize the sinner, care for the needy, and edify the saint. Although these broad categories provide a helpful summary of the church's work, it is somewhat misleading to claim them as the mission of the church. Certainly they are tasks that responsible Christians engage in, but they are more accurately understood as manifestations of a primary mission – to love!

When love is applied, it will take different forms according to the need it encounters. When love comes upon a legitimate need, it seeks to fill it.
- If that need is for the gospel, love preaches.
- If that need is for food, love feeds.
- If that need is for instruction, love teaches.

Every act of kindness is merely an application of love. What is clothing the naked but love? What is contending for the faith but love? What is consoling the bereaved but love?

Let us take for our example the most pressing of all needs, the soul's need for the saving message of Christ. How was God's love demonstrated in this circumstance?

• God the Father applied it when He saw man's helpless condition and sent His Son to die for the sins of mankind (John 3:16).

• God the Son applied it when He came to earth and shed His blood to save humanity (John 15:13).

• God the Spirit applied it when He shared the message of God's love through the preaching and teaching of inspired men (Romans 5:5).

## Holy Spirit Evangelism

A closer examination of the Spirit's role in evangelism is warranted here. Jesus had a *vision* He shared with His disciples before ascending to the Father (Matthew 28:18-20), but He also made a *provision* for the fulfillment of that dream (John 15:26-27). Before undertaking the Great Commission, the apostles were told to wait in Jerusalem for special assistance to help them in their undertaking (Acts 1:7-8). That assistance came in dramatic fashion on the day of Pentecost when God's messengers were baptized in the Holy Spirit. The involvement of the Spirit in the conversion of 3,000 on Pentecost was unmistakable. Peter's message was not only inspired but also confirmed by impressive miracles.

But does the Spirit remain an integral partner in the conversion process today? Jesus taught that the Spirit's job was to convict the world of sin, righteousness and judgment (John 16:8-11). Because the Bible is inspired (Hebrews 4:12), whenever an honest, searching heart comes in contact with the Word of God, his spirit is having a life-changing, destiny-altering encounter with the Holy Spirit.

## The Fruitful Evangelist

But the same Spirit that works in the message also works in the life of the messenger. Every Christian is responsible for evangelizing the lost, but the effective evangelist possesses a spirit that is the outflowing of the indwelling Spirit of God. Paul declared, "And because you are sons, God has sent forth the Spirit of His Son into your hearts, crying out, 'Abba, Father!' " (Galatians 4:6). The apostle provided the Galatians with a list of nine character traits that indicate the Holy Spirit is at work in a Christian's life (5:22-23).

Before looking at Paul's catalog of virtues, more consideration should be given to the spiritual concept of fruit bearing. Simply speaking, it is a figure of speech emphasizing the principle of cause and effect. Fruit is used to describe the character and actions that grow out of dominant thoughts. It is what happens when your inside becomes your outside. When the Spirit is absent and all that remains to influence thought and behavior is of the flesh, the product of one's life can be as unsightly as rotting fruit (Galatians 5:19-21). Over time it becomes increasingly clear to careful observers that something is desperately wrong at the core. In contrast, the Spirit-filled Christian enjoys a bountiful harvest of virtue that is vital for reaching others with the gospel. Paul's point is that those who embrace the Spirit's message relate to others in a healthier, holier way. God's Spirit changes not only character but also relationships.

## *Love*

It is no surprise that love heads the list of virtues that show the Spirit's presence in one's life. But think of this trait in terms of the evangelist's work ("evangelist" meaning a contagious Christian, not a professional minister). To succeed, he must genuinely care about people. Those who have tasted Christ's love and have pledged themselves to love others as He loved them will be "fruitful" evangelists indeed. The Spirit enlarges a Christian's heart and directs it to what is most worth loving. Such a person seeks the betterment of the one loved rather than using a person to gratify his own needs. Converts are not notches in the evangelist's belt or trophies to be displayed; they are precious souls who are encouraged to reach their spiritual potential in Christ. The principal way love for God is shown is in caring for those created in His image.

## *Joy*

The eight virtues that follow are the fruit of love, as well as of the Spirit. When love floods the soul, what will be seen? The first facet of a love-saturated life is pure, unadulterated joy. The implications of this holy happiness are far reaching for evangelists because it is only when we are deeply, genuinely happy in our faith that others want to partake of it.

Jesus' desire is for His followers to know "full" joy (John 15:11). The world may offer occasions of joy, but only Jesus can provide a joy so durable that it can coexist with sorrow. God's joy is resilient because it is not dependent on changing circumstances but on an abiding relationship. It is interesting that "joy" comes from the same Greek root word as "grace." Christian joy is grounded in a loving relationship with God, which was made possible by His mercy. It is that relationship that the evangelist shares with others. Those who talk of such a bond but show no evidence of experiencing it will have difficulty convincing others of its benefit for their lives.

The only limit on the joy a person can know in this lifetime is set by the boundaries of his heart. Love capacity determines joy capacity. If I do not care about you, I cannot take much pleasure in your blessings and accomplishments. When you are dear to me, my joy increases with every good thing that happens in your life (Romans 12:15). Because God's love is as big as the world (John 3:16), His joy is limitless. The more we love like God, the more boundless our joy. One cannot have more joy than love. Therefore, the bigger the heart, the greater its happiness.

## *Peace*

Love-soaked souls also possess an inner peace that helps them remain poised in times of stress and conflict. Effective evangelists have an aura of confidence that comes from drenching their minds in God's Word. This enlightenment of the Spirit allows them to face reality squarely but with calm assurance. God's forgiveness, fellowship and faithfulness provide them with inner strength to do His will despite incredible obstacles. They have:

• *Peace in Purity*. They are bold because they know their sins are truly forgiven. The Spirit has borne witness with their spirit that they are indeed children of God (Romans 8:16-18).

• *Peace in Power*. They are courageous because they know they are not alone. The Spirit has assured them of strength beyond themselves to handle any problem, bear any trial, and resist any temptation (Philippians 4:13).

• *Peace in Promises*. They are brave because they know whose they are and what He has promised. The Spirit has revealed that God will vindicate their faith and right every wrong they have suffered in His name (Romans 8:31-39).

But there is another dimension of peace that must not be overlooked. It is the peacefulness of the soul that knows faith does not rest on philosophical or theological speculation. It is the serenity that comes from simple reliance on straightforward New Testament teaching. This uncomplicated approach to the Christian religion affords those who embrace it a peace that passes all understanding, for tranquility is inseparable from truth. Those who base their religious beliefs and practices on conjecture cannot have the same peace as one who relies wholly upon that which the Spirit has revealed. Effective evangelists do not engage in guesswork; they speak boldly because of confidence in the sufficiency of Scripture to provide spiritual guidance. Such confidence is rooted in conviction, not consensus. It is the comfort that comes from building one's hope for eternity on the solid rock of Jesus' words (Matthew 7:24-27; Colossians 3:17). This peace is not rooted in intellectual infallibility, but in a loving relationship with One who provides His followers with sufficient knowledge to please Him.

## Longsuffering

A fourth fruit found in Spirit-filled men and women is longsuffering. This quality of forbearance is the opposite of anger and retaliation. When asking people to change at the center of their being, why should one expect this to happen instantaneously? Ought not some resistance be expected? Therefore, it is a mistake to sacrifice future relations with potential converts due to preset timetables that are arbitrary and unrealistic. Those who are patient with people will be successful evangelists. External pressure coerces, but internal pressure converts. People must be given the time and space to think deeply if change is to be lasting.

## Kindness

Kindness is the fifth imprint of the Spirit on a Christian's life. Evangelists who are harsh and abrasive are not following the Spirit's lead. Contending for the faith is not an excuse for contentiousness. It is possible to be firm and kind at the same time, but love and rancor cannot coexist in the same heart. Christians do not tell people off, nor do they pointlessly rub people the wrong way. Instead, they are characterized by the tenderheartedness of Jesus (Matthew 11:29-30). They are friendly and easy to be with. They know how to soften their words without diluting the message and are considerate of others' feelings and needs.

# Goodness

A sixth evidence of the Spirit's work in the human personality is goodness. This trait refers to the practical demonstration of Christian faith. Literally, the word means usable or serviceable. Goodness speaks of a life that is accomplishing the divine purpose for which it was created. Like a tree that bears fruit, or a watch that keeps time, Christians have a God-ordained purpose to fulfill. Evangelists whose lives are filled with goodness reinforce their message. Their praiseworthy lives adorn the doctrine of Christ and make it doubly appealing. When good character produces good works that yield a good name, every obstacle is removed that might hinder a fair hearing of the gospel. If the idea of goodness is still unclear, study the lives of Barnabas (Acts 11:24) and Dorcas (9:36), who are commended because of the goodness of their hearts, words and deeds.

# Faithfulness

Faithfulness is the seventh attribute of a love-based life. In a world characterized by fickleness, a person who says what he means and means what he says will make an impression on others. Spirit-led people are honest, trustworthy and loyal. These traits significantly increase opportunities to influence others in a positive way. Therefore, Christians whose lives demonstrate spiritual consistency are more effective in outreach than those who make sporadic attempts to live their faith.

For example, marital fidelity is central to credibility. Why should one trust an evangelist who professes love for him if that person has betrayed the mate he publicly vowed to love and cherish before all others? Reliability in fulfilling financial and work-related responsibilities also gives credence to the gospel message. Why trust the words of one who has proven himself untrustworthy? Faithfulness should also produce an uncompromising commitment to protect the reputation of others, especially when they are not present to protect themselves. Dependability in defending others from slander or misrepresentations garners well-deserved respect.

# Gentleness

Nowhere is the Spirit more obvious in a person's life than in a bearing of gentleness. Prolific evangelists are not conceited or combative, but humble toward their fellowman. They know that whatever goodness exists in their own lives should be attributed to God's power working within them. They understand that a condescending word or tone is unlikely to accomplish God's purpose. Evangelism is not for the proud or self-righteous; it is for those who have a keen awareness of their own weakness and failures. It is for those who know that Satan is the adversary rather than the one who struggles with sin. Gentleness levels the relationship and makes others feel comfortable. It sets them at ease where they do not have equal knowledge of the Bible. It invites them to let down their defenses because no one has come to condemn them. Gentleness is disarming because it lets people know they will not be mocked, manipulated or maligned. It establishes a trusting environment where dignity is respected regardless of serious differences. This non-threatening approach creates an atmosphere of openness conducive to real learning and transformation.

# *Self-Control*

Self-control is the final mark of love from Paul's list of crops harvested from the fertile soil of a Spirit-enriched heart. The evangelist is to be living proof of the gospel's power to bring order, sanity and dignity to daily life. When competing urges battle within, it is possible to resist destructive lusts by bringing spiritual desires to the forefront. No longer must one live at the mercy of fleshly appetites and passions. No longer must one submit to mysterious internal forces that bring life to the brink of disaster. In Genesis 1, the Spirit hovered over the deep to bring order out of chaos and prepare a world capable of sustaining life. Today, the Holy Spirit works to bring order to out-of-control lives and make them fit for our own habitation. Self-control evidences a Spirit-induced love for self that prepares a Christian to share God's love with others.

## Walking in the Spirit

In the conclusion to Paul's fruit analogy, he stated, "Against such there is no law" (Galatians 5:22). Laws are typically used to restrict anti-social behavior. When it comes to acquiring Christlike virtues, there is no need for laws to restrain their procurement. Like health, you can never have too much love, nor can you have an excess of God's Spirit. Because each virtue is possessed in relative measure, the key is to walk in the Spirit. To walk means to progress toward a goal, and in our case, the goal is to increase the measure of love we bring to each encounter in life. The point is not sinless perfection but spiritual progression.

If Christians are not reaching out with the gospel of Christ, it is because they are more full of self than Spirit. Evangelism has always had more to do with pneumatology (the study of the Holy Spirit) than methodology. Yet the work of the Spirit is not limited to producing fruitful evangelists in the church. He will make people more effective in every relational endeavor of life. At work, He will produce considerate bosses and conscientious employees. At home, He will produce compassionate spouses and caring parents. Wherever love is applied, it will enhance human relationships and facilitate the accomplishment of shared purposes. Wherever people congregate or collaborate, love will strengthen their bonds and support their aspirations.

## How Does Your Garden Grow?

The difference between a barren life and a bountiful one is the loving Spirit of Christ. Just as plant growth requires an abundant supply of water, so human growth requires a steady supply of God's Spirit. Jesus declared, " 'He who believes in Me, as the Scripture has said, out of his heart will flow rivers of living water.' But this He spoke concerning the Spirit, whom those believing in Him would receive" (John 7:38-39). The heart grows and thrives with love, but without love the heart shrivels and dies.

Unfruitful lives are spiritual deserts devoid of love. They are human wastelands of ruined relationships, lost opportunities and decaying potential. Fruitful lives are spiritual gardens fed by streams of love. They are patches of heaven on earth filled with blossoming friendships, fulfilled dreams and promising possibilities.

Is your life a garden of delight or a desert of desolation? Start walking in the Spirit and begin enjoying the abundant life and satisfying relationships you have always wanted. Your new life is only a step away!

## *Questions*

1. Which fruit of the Spirit enlarges the human heart?

2. Which trait comes from the same root word as "grace"?

3. Which proof of the Spirit provides an aura of confidence?

4. Which spiritual quality is the opposite of anger and retaliation?

5. Which attribute produces consideration for the feelings and needs of others?

6. Which characteristic refers to being usable or serviceable?

7. Which asset of the Spirit is manifested in marital fidelity?

8. Which trait levels relationships and makes others feel comfortable?

9. Which virtue proves the gospel's power to bring order, sanity and dignity to life?

10. If the point of Christian living is not sinless perfection, then what is it?

## *Discussion Questions*

1. What is the mission of Christ's Church?

2. What is the role of the Holy Spirit in evangelism today?

3. What does it mean to walk in the Spirit?

# Love Quest Survey
## Pursuing a God-Shaped Heart

### Love More                    (Rate your progress this week)

My love skills (behaviors that make me MORE loving)      Better – Worse
1. Honesty (realistic, truthful, self-aware)             ❏      ❏
2. Empathy (thoughtful, compassionate, kind, forgiving)  ❏      ❏
3. Responsibility (accountable, reliable, disciplined)   ❏      ❏

My love opportunities – Mark 12:30-31
• God (loving enthusiastically – without reservation)    Better – Worse
1. With all my heart (warm, affectionate love)           ❏      ❏
2. With all my mind (intelligent, informed love)         ❏      ❏
3. With all my strength (energetic, devoted love)        ❏      ❏
4. With all my soul (integrated, holistic love)          ❏      ❏
• Others (loving empathetically – doing good, not harm)  Better – Worse

| | Better | Worse | | Better | Worse |
|---|---|---|---|---|---|
| 1. My mate | ❏ | ❏ | 5. My child | ❏ | ❏ |
| 2. My best friend | ❏ | ❏ | 6. My boss | ❏ | ❏ |
| 3. My co-worker | ❏ | ❏ | 7. My neighbor | ❏ | ❏ |
| 4. My enemy | ❏ | ❏ | 8. My encounters with strangers | ❏ | ❏ |

• Self (loving effectively – bringing out my best self)  Better – Worse
1. My body (caring for my physical needs and health)        ❏   ❏
2. My heart (caring for my emotional needs and self-esteem) ❏   ❏
3. My mind (caring for my intellectual needs and growth)    ❏   ❏
4. My soul (caring for my spiritual needs and destiny)      ❏   ❏

### Sin Less                    (Rate your progress this week)

• My sin snares (behaviors that make me LESS loving)       Better – Worse
1. Irrationality (unrealistic, unaware, untruthful)          ❏   ❏
2. Fabricating (exaggerating, demonizing, romanticizing)     ❏   ❏
3. Insensitivity (uncaring, unkind, unmindful)               ❏   ❏
4. Irresponsibility (undisciplined, unreliable, unaccountable) ❏ ❏
• My sin challenges (ways I hurt the people I profess to love) Better – Worse
1. Tongue (gossiping, criticizing, blaming, lying)           ❏   ❏
2. Temper (anger, negativity, intimidation)                  ❏   ❏
3. Temptations (lust, pride, selfishness, laziness)          ❏   ❏

### My Loving Journal (developing my love-consciousness)
• I felt loved last week when …
• Loving choices I made last week:
• Unloving choices I made last week:
• This week I will love more by …
• This week I will sin less by …

# The Loving God

*"He who does not love does not know God,*
*for God is love." – 1 John 4:8*

---

The loved-based life requires more than information and determination. It takes grace! Grace is resilient love, and its hardiness is most evident in response to unrequited love. It is through grace that the celestial and terrestrial worlds come together so that God's will is done on earth as in heaven. Without mercy there could be no mingling of worlds, merging of minds, blending of wills, and fusing of hearts. Without forgiveness, intimacy is impossible. Grace paves the way for salvation and transformation. It accomplishes what knowledge and willpower alone can never do. Without grace, every relationship crumbles.

Grace is God-glue, a spiritual adhesive to be liberally applied where the bond of love has been weakened by sin. In chapter 12, we see God's grace at work as He keeps His promises to unfaithful people. In chapter 13, we see God's mercy at work as He models unity to selfish people. God's faithfulness sparks hope, and His oneness inspires harmony. Sampling these gracious gifts creates a hunger for the love-based life. Therefore, the most important factor in spiritual health and loving relationships is to know God. Those who taste His grace and savor His love are well on their way to loving more and sinning less.

# Chapter 12

# Love Motivated:
# Hope

*"The grand essentials of happiness are: something to do,*
*something to love, and something to hope for."*
*– Allan K. Chalmers*

<hr>

A ll human behavior is motivated by physiological or psychological forces. Therefore, change is the consequence of the mind and body being programmed differently. Transformation comes from information. Sometimes that information is provided subconsciously, as in the case of physical growth. For instance, it does not take deep concentration for an adolescent boy to outgrow his clothes. Some changes occur naturally; others require conscious effort, as in the case of spiritual growth.

The gospel contains the genetic code of Christ to reproduce His love in the lives of His followers (Galatians 2:20). However, the spiritual DNA contained in Christ's blood must be infused by faith. The story of Christ's love on the cross must be believed to be beneficial. When this occurs, it not only liberates from sin but also stimulates constructive change in behavior and relationships. This process is well-described in Peter's second epistle:

> Simon Peter, a bondservant and apostle of Jesus Christ, to those who have obtained like precious faith with us by the righteousness of our God and Savior Jesus Christ: Grace and peace be multiplied to you in the knowledge of God and

of Jesus our Lord, as His divine power has given to us all things that pertain to life and godliness, through the knowledge of Him who called us by glory and virtue, by which have been given to us exceedingly great and precious promises, that through these you may be partakers of the divine nature, having escaped the corruption that is in the world through lust (2 Peter 1:1-4).

Peter revealed that the knowledge of Christ literally multiplies the life-enhancing effects of grace and peace. When a believer embraces biblical teaching, the power contained in God's Word is released to do its work. Scripture contains spiritual energy like the life-force that enables cells to replicate. As Christians grow, they partake of the divine nature, and the family resemblance becomes increasingly obvious to those who monitor their development.

Peter goes on to identify the virtues that evidence spiritual growth and health: "But for this very reason, giving all diligence, add to your faith virtue, to virtue knowledge, to knowledge self-control, to self-control perseverance, to perseverance godliness, to godliness brotherly kindness, and to brotherly kindness love" (2 Peter 1:5-7). Christians are to give diligence to add each of this traits to their lives. The word "diligence" suggests that mindfulness is mandatory. Attention and exertion are vital to growth. But what is the dynamic that sparks and sustains this drive?

## *The Power of Love*

Love is the highest and strongest motivator of human behavior. Love changes attitudes, encourages effort, sustains activity, fosters cooperation and bonds human beings in wholesome ways. It is a force so powerful it can override primal instincts for self-preservation. Jesus' love led Him to surrender His life on the cross to save lost souls from eternal punishment.

Conduct unmotivated by the need to give and receive love is abnormal, and psychologists classify it as mental illness (attachment disorders and sociopathy). Conditions of this kind may be genetic or trauma induced, but sin is also capable of interfering with the natural motivating power of love by confusing selfish acts with caring conduct (Romans 1:28-31). For example, casual sex can be viewed as a demonstration of affection, but it is a dehumanizing act and an affront to love. Similarly, drug users experience a kind of camaraderie, but their common weakness undermines and damages their relationships. A full and satisfying life requires more than mutual indulgence in passing pleasure. True joy requires healthy togetherness that brings out the best in others. This level of joy, of course, requires love.

## A Theory of Love

The motivational power of love can be illustrated by "Expectancy Theory." The basic idea behind this theory is that if you believe you will be sufficiently rewarded for a particular behavior then you will be inclined to act accordingly. Three questions must be answered to assess the strength of motivational incentives.

• Can I trust the person to do what he or she has promised?
• Can I do what the person asked to obtain what was promised?
• Do I want to do what was requested to receive the promise?

For instance, if you are told you will be given a million dollars to jump off your roof, you might do it if you believed the person had the money and would make good on the promise. But few would be inclined to jump off a cliff, regardless of the dollar amount (unless provided with equipment to survive the rapid descent). When considering God's directives, one asks similar questions.

• Can I trust God?
• Can I do what God asks?
• Is it worth it?

One who answers these questions affirmatively may be described as hopeful. Biblical hope is not wishful thinking or wild speculation; rather, it is confident expectation. It is the belief that God is not only all powerful but also all loving. Disobedience stems from a lack of confidence in God. The fruit of doubt is despair and dysfunction, whereas the fruit of hope is effectiveness and eternal life. There is no middle ground. To understand how the anticipation of positive outcomes blesses believers, each of the questions discussed should be considered in more detail.

# Is God Trustworthy?

God's trustworthiness is a constant theme throughout the Bible. In Deuteronomy, Moses retraced the history of God's care for His people to inspire loyalty to His covenant (Deuteronomy 1:6–4:49). In his farewell address, Joshua reassured a wavering nation that God kept every promise made to them and would do the same in the future (Joshua 23:14). Solomon also defended God's integrity as One who keeps His word without fail (1 Kings 8:56).

In Hebrews, saints who were teetering on apostasy were reminded that God would not fail to reward them if they remained faithful (4:1; 10:36; 11:6). God's loyalty is inseparable from His love. He can be depended on precisely because of His unwavering devotion to His people. Love, therefore, serves as the foundation for motivating positive change in human behavior.

Paul championed God's credibility in his epistle to the Romans. He assured his readers that those who put their faith in God would never be disappointed (5:5). He appealed to their experience with God's Word as indisputable evidence of His reliability (12:2). Whenever Scripture is believed and obeyed, it is shown to be beneficial.

The success of Paul's ministry was a direct result of his confidence in God's faithfulness. He explained, "I know whom I have believed and am persuaded that He is able to keep what I have committed to Him until that Day" (2 Timothy 1:12). Paul knew he could count on God because he knew how much God cared for him (Romans 8:35-39). Simply put, those who love most can be trusted most, and those who love least can be trusted least.

Christians can trust their heavenly Father to
• Forgive their sins (1 John 1:9).
• Hear their prayers (1 Peter 5:7).
• Guard their hearts (Philippians 4:7).
• Renew their minds (Romans 12:2).
• Complete their characters (James 1:4).
• Bless their endeavors (Romans 8:28).
• Raise their bodies (1 Thessalonians 4:16).
• Save their souls (Jude 24).

The fact that God does not grant every request made of Him does not mean He is lacking in love, power or faithfulness. The Lord never promised that marriages and banks would never fail. He never pledged that stocks and soufflés would never fall. Because God will not violate our free will or keep us from experiencing the uncertainties of life does not mean He does not care. In other words, God never said he would give His children everything they want, but He positively guaranteed He would provide everything they need (Psalm 23:1; Matthew 7:7-11).

**God never promised ... But He has promised ...**

Tomorrow ... Eternal Life

No trouble ... No temptation we cannot bear

No weakness ... To renew our strength

No sickness ... A resurrection body

A new house ... A home in heaven

Earthly wealth ... Riches in faith

Worldly inheritance ... A heavenly reward

Diamonds and pearls ... A crown of life

No heartache ... Comfort for our hearts

No loneliness ... Never to leave or forsake us

No sadness ... To wipe away every tear

## *Can I Do What God Asks?*

Even great leaders in the Bible have doubted their ability to fulfill God's expectations. When called by the Lord, Moses repeatedly argued that God's demands exceeded his capabilities. In response, the Lord patiently addressed each objection to bolster his confidence. Elijah attempted to evade his responsibility by fleeing into the wilderness to escape the reach of Jezebel. God comforted the discouraged prophet and assigned him new tasks to perform. This was God's way of expressing His belief in Elijah's ability to get the job done. At first, Gideon shrugged off the angel's pronouncement that he was a mighty man of valor who would deliver Israel from her enemies. Through multiple miracles, God convinced Gideon that he would be used for great purposes.

These men learned that competence cannot be limited to one's intellect, energy or skill. Spiritual sufficiency is ultimately determined by the state of one's relationship with God. As Paul declared, "I can do all things through Christ who strengthens me" (Philippians 4:13). Christians possess an adequacy that reaches beyond their own natural reserves. This promise does not guarantee technical competency for any undertaking in life (rocket science or brain surgery), but it does guarantee that God will provide whatever is needed to do what He wants or become what He asks. In most cases, a miraculous provision is not necessary; rather, it is the strengthening of a saint's resolve (1 Corinthians 15:58). Such was the case with Paul's charge to the Ephesians: "Finally, my brethren, be strong in the Lord and in the power of His might" (Ephesians 6:10). Fear and doubt rob Christians of the courage they need to accomplish God's purpose for their lives. Love links Christians to real power beyond themselves – divine power!

## *Is It Worth It?*

What are the consequences of receiving and returning God's love? Satan would have people believe the result is unnecessary self-denial and misery. He tries to make them feel foolish for placing their trust in Christ and His Word. The result of this psychological shift is sin. In the garden, Satan undermined Adam's and Eve's confidence in God's love for them. When their faith failed, so did their love for each other. As a result, they disobeyed God and damaged their own relationship.

To counter Satan's efforts, God has filled the Bible with incentives for trusting Him and complying with His Word. That is why preachers exhort as well as instruct. Spiritual leaders supply hope by highlighting the rewards of faithfulness sprinkled throughout the pages of Scripture. Some blessings will be received in the future; others can be enjoyed now.

• *Delayed Benefits.* Delayed benefits include heaven, health and harmony.

– Heaven – There is the promise of a new home that saints will enjoy throughout eternity. Biblical metaphors provide assurance that this dwelling place will be superior to anything in man's previous experience. Heaven will be a place of surpassing beauty and bounty.

– Health – There is a guarantee of a new body that is not subject to disease and death. Terrestrial bodies will be exchanged for celestial ones impervious to sickness and suffering.

– Harmony – There is the assurance of improved relationships among all of heaven's citizens. The sin and selfishness that interfered with relationships on earth will be forgotten in this love-perfected realm. All the adversity and anxiety of this present life will be a distant memory because of God's wonderful provision.

• *Immediate Benefits.* Still, all the blessings of obedience are not deferred to another time and place. Christians are recipients of God's goodness at the very instant they conform their lives to His will. Better fitness, higher self-esteem and increased joy are a few of the benefits that derive from wholehearted devotion to God.

– Better Fitness – From a pragmatic viewpoint, improved health is a natural consequence of living in harmony with the world as God created it. Sin has physical as well as spiritual symptoms. It can sidetrack a person from caring for his body as much as his soul. Insomnia, malnutrition and a variety of stress-related disorders can be attributed to sinful diversions such as pleasure-seeking or worldly preoccupations such as materialism. Even plain old worry can produce serious health complications. It drains a person's energy and distracts him from taking constructive action to alleviate problems. Sin does not account for all illness, but it contributes to a multitude of infirmities by keeping people from exercising control over their lives.

– Higher Self-Esteem – Another immediate benefit of submitting to God's will is the inner satisfaction one derives from fulfilling his spiritual potential. Paul remarked, "For we are His workmanship, created in Christ Jesus for good works, which God prepared beforehand that we should walk in them" (Ephesians 2:10). When a person feels useful, it produces a positive swell of emotion that comes from an approving conscience. Human beings were made by God to love and serve one another. That is why self-indulgence is always disappointing. Satisfaction comes in direct proportion to the contribution one makes to the lives of others.

– Increased Joy – In addition to the natural joy one derives from serving others through good works comes the pleasure of knowing that God is pleased with such acts of compassion. Just as parents delight in each phase of a child's development, the heavenly Father is thrilled when His children experience new stages of spiritual growth. Spiritual maturity is demonstrated in increasing responsibility. The more reliable one becomes, the more heaven rejoices.

The effects of sin are injurious because sinful behavior is based on false assumptions about the way life works. Truth liberates a person from the harmful consequences of conduct founded on limited or corrupted knowledge. God works providentially on behalf of believers, but it is their responsibility to work in concert with the laws He enacted to govern the cosmos. Those who consistently defy those laws will suffer the consequences of their ignorance or rebellion. Those who cooperate with these universal laws enjoy greater happiness and success in life.

## Can God Be Pleased?

It is wrong to assume that God cannot be pleased with anything less than perfection (1 Thessalonians 4:1). Such a notion would drive honest souls to the brink of despair. It is healthier to say that the more a person strives to become like Christ, the more joy he brings his heavenly Father. Faithful and functional lives are a delight to the Lord because He hates to see people suffer needlessly or inflict pointless pain in others' lives. Conversely, He is overjoyed to observe Christians caring for one another's needs and reaching out to help those trapped in sin and selfishness.

God is concerned with the direction of a person's life. No one ever attains full Christlikeness on earth. No one ever achieves complete holiness until heaven. Yet God is pleased when His people draw near to Him (James 4:8). Even the admission of sin is lauded as a move in the right direction (Matthew 5:4). Growth makes God glad because growth is measured in conformity to Christ, who models the true meaning of love.

## Motives for Christian Maturity

• *Negative.* The reasons for Christian living are nearly boundless. From a negative standpoint, who wants to spend eternity in torment (2 Corinthians 5:10)? The weeping and gnashing of teeth associated with hell suggest a combination of physical suffering and the emotional pain of regret. The story of sin is a story of wastefulness: wasted possessions and potential (Luke 15:13; Matthew 25:24-30); wasted time and opportunity (Ephesians 5:15-16; Romans 2:4-11). It is the story of a life lived without consideration for God or others. Yet fear of hell is incapable of sustaining the soul. It can spark interest in eternal things and initiate religious activity, but it cannot inspire genuine righteousness. God is concerned with motives, not just deeds, and dread of punishment alone has never saved a soul from hell.

• *Positive.* From a positive perspective, Christian living is desirable because no one wants to miss out on the rewards God has prepared for the faithful (Titus 2:11-15; John 14:1-4). The delights of heaven are definitely worth pursuing, but the highest inducement for living a Christian life is love. When called to account for the motive behind his ministry, Paul wrote, "For the love of Christ compels us" (2 Corinthians 5:14). Those who grasp the meaning of the cross are overwhelmed by the immensity of Jesus' love. Paul said there is real power in it to sustain a godly life. Those who know Jesus' love live for others. His love stirs saints to share what they have received. It rouses remnants of compassion from hidden recesses of the heart. Christ's love sets the soul aflame with a devotion to others that is incomprehensible to those who have not experienced it. Those who have wept at the cross and been bathed in Christ's blood do not love this world or live for it. They have a higher, better, more enduring reason for living.

## *Love Is Number One*

Love is the strongest incentive for personal change. It is also the key to helping others make meaningful improvements in their own lives. How does a husband aid his wife in overcoming her addiction to alcohol? How does a parent assist a child who underachieves due to low self-esteem? How does an elder reclaim a backsliding brother? Nagging, berating and threatening seldom accomplish their intended purpose. Although the particulars may differ, the most conducive climate for change is always the safety of a loving relationship (1 Corinthians 13:7). Love does not mean approving or condoning bad behavior. It does mean humbly and patiently supporting people's efforts toward constructive change. It is reminding them of God's love and the guarantee of His assistance in overcoming the most stubborn sin. Many motives are good, but the greatest of incentives – bar none – is love (v. 13).

# Questions

1. What is the result of the mind or body being informed differently?

2. What multiplies the life-enhancing effects of grace and peace?

3. What is the highest and strongest motivator of human behavior?

4. What theory demonstrates the motivational power of love?

5. What must preachers supply in addition to ethical instruction?

6. What makes God glad?

7. The story of sin is the story of what?

8. What are three delayed benefits of Christian living?

9. What is a consequence of living in harmony with the world as God created it?

10. Name three things that seldom accomplish their purpose in producing change?

## Discussion Questions

1. Why can those who love most be trusted most?

2. Why has the dread of hell alone never saved a soul from hell?

3. How does love motivate positive change?

# Love Quest Survey
## Pursuing a God-Shaped Heart

## Love More       (Rate your progress this week)

My love skills (behaviors that make me MORE loving)    Better – Worse

| | Better | Worse |
|---|---|---|
| 1. Honesty (realistic, truthful, self-aware) | ❏ | ❏ |
| 2. Empathy (thoughtful, compassionate, kind, forgiving) | ❏ | ❏ |
| 3. Responsibility (accountable, reliable, disciplined) | ❏ | ❏ |

My love opportunities – Mark 12:30-31

• God (loving enthusiastically – without reservation)    Better – Worse

| | Better | Worse |
|---|---|---|
| 1. With all my heart (warm, affectionate love) | ❏ | ❏ |
| 2. With all my mind (intelligent, informed love) | ❏ | ❏ |
| 3. With all my strength (energetic, devoted love) | ❏ | ❏ |
| 4. With all my soul (integrated, holistic love) | ❏ | ❏ |

• Others (loving empathetically – doing good, not harm)    Better – Worse

| | Better | Worse | | Better | Worse |
|---|---|---|---|---|---|
| 1. My mate | ❏ | ❏ | 5. My child | ❏ | ❏ |
| 2. My best friend | ❏ | ❏ | 6. My boss | ❏ | ❏ |
| 3. My co-worker | ❏ | ❏ | 7. My neighbor | ❏ | ❏ |
| 4. My enemy | ❏ | ❏ | 8. My encounters with strangers | ❏ | ❏ |

• Self (loving effectively – bringing out my best self)    Better – Worse

| | Better | Worse |
|---|---|---|
| 1. My body (caring for my physical needs and health) | ❏ | ❏ |
| 2. My heart (caring for my emotional needs and self-esteem) | ❏ | ❏ |
| 3. My mind (caring for my intellectual needs and growth) | ❏ | ❏ |
| 4. My soul (caring for my spiritual needs and destiny) | ❏ | ❏ |

## Sin Less       (Rate your progress this week)

• My sin snares (behaviors that make me LESS loving)    Better – Worse

| | Better | Worse |
|---|---|---|
| 1. Irrationality (unrealistic, unaware, untruthful) | ❏ | ❏ |
| 2. Fabricating (exaggerating, demonizing, romanticizing) | ❏ | ❏ |
| 3. Insensitivity (uncaring, unkind, unmindful) | ❏ | ❏ |
| 4. Irresponsibility (undisciplined, unreliable, unaccountable) | ❏ | ❏ |

• My sin challenges (ways I hurt the people I profess to love)   Better – Worse

| | Better | Worse |
|---|---|---|
| 1. Tongue (gossiping, criticizing, blaming, lying) | ❏ | ❏ |
| 2. Temper (anger, negativity, intimidation) | ❏ | ❏ |
| 3. Temptations (lust, pride, selfishness, laziness) | ❏ | ❏ |

## My Loving Journal (developing my love-consciousness)

• I felt loved last week when …
• Loving choices I made last week:
• Unloving choices I made last week:
• This week I will love more by …
• This week I will sin less by …

# Chapter 13

# *Love Inspired:*
# Unity

*"This is all that I've known for certain, that God is love." –*
*Søren Kierkegaard*

---

T he study of the Trinity is not just for theologians and seminary students. Understanding God's oneness is vitally important for every
Christian. To understand the relationship between the Father, Son
and Spirit is to understand love.

Paul taught that a Christian's life should adorn the doctrine of God
(Titus 2:10). If the doctrine of God is foremost a message of love, then
adorning that doctrine demands a life of love. Therefore, a better grasp
of God's oneness will help Christians relate effectively, increase their
influence for good, and aid in the salvation of more souls. The more
one loves, the more satisfying and successful life becomes.

## *The Complexity of God*

Most theologians use the word "Trinity" to describe the three-in-one
God; however, the term "Trinity" does not appear in the Bible. It comes
from the Greek word *trinitas,* which means "threeness." The question is whether God can be both three and one at the same time.

Songwriting demonstrates the way various things come together to
make a greater whole. It takes many notes to construct a melody, many

words to compose lyrics, and the combination of melody and lyrics to create a sacred hymn. The complexity of a hymn is mind-boggling when broken down into its constituent parts: letters, language, poetry, music, eye, ear, heart, writer, publisher, printer, binder, distributor, church and the God who is adored.

Just as it would be a mistake to reject the oneness of a hymn because of its complexities, it is also a mistake to reject the oneness of God because of intellectual difficulties. Songs share a oneness of essence and function that makes sense to most people. Although the attributes and actions of God exceed those of created things, it is possible to illustrate that oneness and threeness are not mutually exclusive.

Consider the interaction of brush, paint and canvas to make a masterpiece or the merging of body, chassis and engine to form a car. Even more dynamic is the cooperation of orchestra members to perform a symphony or members of a sports team to produce a championship. Unity of purpose draws people closer together as they pursue common goals. Although the glory of the Godhead transcends that of musicians, artists, athletes and engineers, there is a similarity in their cohesiveness and the bonding power of committed, creative love. Labors of love link hearts both human and divine.

## Godhead in the Old Testament

The combination of God's threeness and oneness is apparent in many biblical texts. In the Old Testament, the most commonly quoted passage espousing the oneness of God is Deuteronomy 6:4: "Hear, O Israel: The Lord our God, the Lord is one!" The fact that God is one is not open to debate. The manner in which people should understand this oneness has been a matter of discussion through the centuries.

Although the Trinity is not fully revealed until the New Testament, there are many Old Testament texts that hint at the concept. For instance, the Hebrew word *Elohim* (God) takes a plural form. In the Genesis account of creation, God says, "Let Us make man in Our image, according to Our likeness" (Genesis 1:26). A similar passage is found in the narrative surrounding the building of the tower of Babel. God said, "Come, let Us go down, and there confuse their language" (11:7). The use of the plural pronoun could be a literary device comparable to the royal or editorial "we" in English. Still, it is also the kind of communication consistent with biblical teaching about the shared role of the Godhead in creation.

The Hebrew word for "one" in Deuteronomy 6:4 is *echad,* which suggests oneness in unity rather than in isolation. *Echad* is frequently used to express a complex oneness. For example, when the spies came back from the land of Canaan, they brought with them an *echad* of grapes as proof of the land's fruitfulness. The reference is not to a single grape but to a bunch of grapes. Moses said the Israelites responded with "one" voice as they entered a covenant relationship with God (Exodus 24:3). The unity they enjoyed was psychological and operational, not merely mathematical or physical.

## Godhead in the New Testament

In the New Testament, the idea of the Godhead is far more developed. On one hand, there is a clear affirmation of the oneness of God established in the Shema. Paul wrote, "[T]here is no God but one" (1 Corinthians 8:4), and James concurred by declaring, "You believe that God is one. You do well" (James 2:19).

On the other hand, the New Testament clearly attributes divinity to Jesus and the Holy Spirit. Jesus' eternal nature is established in John 1:1-2, and His divine power was evidenced in the miracles He performed over nature. The Holy Spirit is said to be infinite in regard to time (Hebrews 9:14), space (Psalm 139:7-10), knowledge (1 Corinthians 2:10-11), and power (Luke 1:35).

The question is: "How can there be one God when the Bible plainly speaks of three beings who possess divine characteristics?" Some deny full divinity to Jesus and the Holy Spirit. Others claim that God revealed Himself to the world in three different forms to fulfill different purposes. The real answer lies in a fuller understanding of the idea of oneness.

## Form Versus Function

Although Father, Son and Spirit clearly partake of the same substance and characteristics, the emphasis of Scripture is on their relationship with one another in the context of caring for mankind. Every member of the Godhead was present and active in creation (Genesis 1:1; John 1:3; Job 33:4). Each played a critical role in the incarnation (Luke 1:35; Galatians 4:4). All were present at the inauguration of Jesus' public ministry (Matthew 3:16-17). Father, Son and Spirit each played a crucial part in the atonement (Hebrews 9:14). Likewise, the resurrection of Christ was attributed to every member of the Godhead (John 10:17-18; Acts 2:32; Romans 1:4).

It is in salvation history that Christians truly begin to comprehend the oneness of God. As His people, we have been "elected[ed] according to the foreknowledge of God the Father, in sanctification of the Spirit, for obedience and sprinkling the blood of Jesus Christ" (1 Peter 1:2). We are sent into the world to "make disciples of all nations, baptizing them in the name of the Father and of the Son and of the Holy Spirit" (Matthew 28:19). But what are the practical implications of God's oneness when it comes to living the Christian life? If believers are ignorant of this doctrine or reject it outright, is anything lost? Indeed, there is a high price to pay.

## A Model Relationship

It may be argued that nothing is really lost because the Bible accentuates the value of love in many passages. Yet what is lost is the power of the message.

• In the home, parents can instruct their children on the importance of right behavior but lecturing cannot compare with living it in their presence.

• In school, teachers can read students the definition of a "gorge" but that hardly measures up to taking a field trip to the Grand Canyon.

• In the church, it is one thing to look up "love" in a lexicon but another thing to witness the gracious love that flows between members of the Godhead. It is by coming into the presence of love that one best internalizes love.

The oneness of God is the story of a perfect relationship. It is a heavenly paradigm of healthy interaction. It is a model for what Christians are to strive to become. Reflecting this unity is the goal of God's people. It is becoming by grace what God is by nature. Sin, on the other hand, interferes with this connection. It ruins relationships and mars

God's image within people. Sin is impersonal or anti-social behavior and destroys the capacity for intimacy and fellowship.

• *Oneness in Marriage.* A study of God's oneness is more beneficial for husbands and wives than any marriage enrichment seminar. A husband who lords his authority over his spouse does not understand the intention of God in providing functional headship for the home. There is a oneness and a twoness about married couples that is modeled after the loving relationship within the Godhead.

"Therefore a man shall leave his father and mother and be joined to his wife, and they shall become one flesh" (Genesis 2:24). Once again, the word for "one" is *echad.* The husband and wife do not become one person, but their yoking makes it impossible to consider one without the other. They are equal in nature, worth, dignity and standing before God (Galatians 3:26-28), yet they carry out distinctive roles for the good of the family, church and community.

Couples would do well to reread the account of Christ, coequal with God, who emptied Himself of outward manifestations of His divinity in order to redeem mankind. The Son's submissive role did not make Him less than the Father. In fact, the willingness of Jesus to serve others was evidence of His greatness. Power struggles in the home indicate that family members have lost touch with the meaning of the Godhead. Husbands and wives are to submit to one another within the framework of their unique roles by putting consideration for the other's needs above personal wants.

• *Oneness in Ministry.* Similarly, elders and deacons can look to God's oneness for a better understanding of leadership in the church. Elders who equate authority with imposing their will have much to learn. Likewise, deacons who consider their roles to be inferior to those of elders have a distorted view of their work. There is a functional difference between elders and deacons, but one is not greater or lesser than the other in the eyes of the Lord. Each fulfills his God-ordained task with respect for others at the forefront of all that he does. Their work is complementary, not competitive.

Father, Son and Spirit are one in essence, but the emphasis of Scripture is upon their oneness in action. In other words, they are not only equal but also united. The oneness of the Godhead encourages all people of faith to be unified in three vital ways: compassion (caring deeply for one another), commission (elevating saving souls to the pinnacle of their concerns), and cooperation (foregoing personal preferences for the good of the church).

When Christians do these things, they are reflecting the glory of God. Biblical writers have expressed this principle in numerous ways. To the Corinthians, Paul said that Christians are interconnected parts of the body of Christ. To the Ephesians, Paul wrote that Christians are living stones joined together to make up the true temple of God. The concept of many becoming one – not just any one but a Godlike one – is the heart of the Christian faith.

## *An Exalted Purpose*

There are aspects of the Godhead which fall into the realm of God's private knowledge (Deuteronomy 29:29), but what Christians need to know, and what He intended them to know, is within the intellectual grasp of ordinary people. The mind cannot fully comprehend the organic oneness of the infinite God, but those who conclude that a study of the Godhead detracts from the purpose of the gospel simply do not understand what that purpose is. God's oneness instructs believers on how to relate more effectively in the home, church and community. More importantly, it inspires Christians to interact with others in a healthier and holier way. What this means is that those with the greatest appreciation for the Godhead love more, sin less and relate best! What higher purpose could there possibly be?

## *Unlocking Happiness*

As this book closes, remember that the key that unlocks the vast treasure vault of God's Word now rests in your hands. That key is the simple truth that "God is love." Grasping this fact opens the door to a fuller life, richer relationships and a closer walk with God. A significant life is not about career, wealth, power or fame; a truly satisfying life is about intimacy: knowing and being known by God, loving and being loved by others.

Therefore, love is no mere component of the Christian faith, but the foundational concept upon which all biblical teaching rests.

Love is …
• The conclusion of Scripture.
• The capstone of God's commandments.
• The chief proof of discipleship.
• The crowning law of laws.

Love is the organizing principle of God's Word and, consequently, of a meaningful life. When a person lacks this knowledge, religion is a mystery and a burden rather than a blessing. Seeking moral purity apart from purer love is pure folly, and pursuing abundant life without a loving life is a waste of life.

So now that you know the greatest secret in the world, what remains to be seen is the difference it will make in your world.

Although perfect relationships are a childish fantasy, healthy relationships are possible and occur every day in the world around you. People learn, grow, forgive and resolve problems all the time. The question is, "What will you do with your newfound knowledge?" My hope is that you will join those who are committed to making the world a more loving place in Jesus' name. For without love, what is there to believe in? And without love, what is there to hope for?

Christianity contains various virtues and countless commandments, but let there be no doubt that "the greatest of these is love."

## *Questions*

1. What does the Greek word for "Trinity" mean?

2. What are some examples of threeness and oneness?

3. What Hebrew word was used to express complex oneness?

4. What Hebrew name for God takes the plural form?

5. When a man leaves home and cleaves to his wife, what do they become?

6. What New Testament writer said, "There is no God but one"?

7. What New Testament writer said, "You believe that God is one; you do well"?

8. What image did Paul use to convey the idea of Christian oneness to the Corinthians?

9. What image did Paul use to convey the idea of Christian oneness to the Ephesians?

10. Name three things in which Christians should be unified?

## *Discussion Questions*

1. Why is it important to understand the oneness of God?

2. How does this understanding assist families? Churches?

3. How have you benefited from the series of lessons contained in this book?

# Love Quest Survey
## Pursuing a God-Shaped Heart

### Love More     (Rate your progress this week)

My love skills (behaviors that make me MORE loving)

| | Better | Worse |
|---|---|---|
| 1. Honesty (realistic, truthful, self-aware) | ☐ | ☐ |
| 2. Empathy (thoughtful, compassionate, kind, forgiving) | ☐ | ☐ |
| 3. Responsibility (accountable, reliable, disciplined) | ☐ | ☐ |

My love opportunities – Mark 12:30-31

• God (loving enthusiastically – without reservation)

| | Better | Worse |
|---|---|---|
| 1. With all my heart (warm, affectionate love) | ☐ | ☐ |
| 2. With all my mind (intelligent, informed love) | ☐ | ☐ |
| 3. With all my strength (energetic, devoted love) | ☐ | ☐ |
| 4. With all my soul (integrated, holistic love) | ☐ | ☐ |

• Others (loving empathetically – doing good, not harm)

| | Better | Worse | | Better | Worse |
|---|---|---|---|---|---|
| 1. My mate | ☐ | ☐ | 5. My child | ☐ | ☐ |
| 2. My best friend | ☐ | ☐ | 6. My boss | ☐ | ☐ |
| 3. My co-worker | ☐ | ☐ | 7. My neighbor | ☐ | ☐ |
| 4. My enemy | ☐ | ☐ | 8. My encounters with strangers | ☐ | ☐ |

• Self (loving effectively – bringing out my best self)

| | Better | Worse |
|---|---|---|
| 1. My body (caring for my physical needs and health) | ☐ | ☐ |
| 2. My heart (caring for my emotional needs and self-esteem) | ☐ | ☐ |
| 3. My mind (caring for my intellectual needs and growth) | ☐ | ☐ |
| 4. My soul (caring for my spiritual needs and destiny) | ☐ | ☐ |

### Sin Less     (Rate your progress this week)

• My sin snares (behaviors that make me LESS loving)

| | Better | Worse |
|---|---|---|
| 1. Irrationality (unrealistic, unaware, untruthful) | ☐ | ☐ |
| 2. Fabricating (exaggerating, demonizing, romanticizing) | ☐ | ☐ |
| 3. Insensitivity (uncaring, unkind, unmindful) | ☐ | ☐ |
| 4. Irresponsibility (undisciplined, unreliable, unaccountable) | ☐ | ☐ |

• My sin challenges (ways I hurt the people I profess to love)

| | Better | Worse |
|---|---|---|
| 1. Tongue (gossiping, criticizing, blaming, lying) | ☐ | ☐ |
| 2. Temper (anger, negativity, intimidation) | ☐ | ☐ |
| 3. Temptations (lust, pride, selfishness, laziness) | ☐ | ☐ |

## My Loving Journal (developing my love-consciousness)
• I felt loved last week when …
• Loving choices I made last week:
• Unloving choices I made last week:
• This week I will love more by …
• This week I will sin less by …

# The Mystery of Sin

A lthough the title of this book emphasizes the centrality of love in the Christian life, the corollary to such a study was an investigation of the corresponding theme of sin, the nemesis of love. What is sin? How does it work? What are its effects? What is its cure? One cannot truly appreciate love without asking these questions.

To understand the periodic failure of human love, it was necessary to undertake a careful study of the psychology of sin. "Psychology" is a scientific term for the study of behavior and its underlying mental processes. "Sin" is a spiritual designation for irresponsible behavior that results from misuse of those processes.

By blending the language of theology and psychology, this book aims to provide Christians with a better understanding of the dynamics influencing human conduct and the neverending struggle between good and bad urges. By explaining biblical terminology in behavioral language, I hope that readers have gained new insights into what goes on behind the scenes of conscious activity. My goal was to expose Satan's duplicitous methods, demystify temptation, and shed light upon the deeper meaning of faith, hope and love.

Those who gain a fuller understanding of the inner workings of sin have a strategic advantage over those who lack this information. Knowledge is power! Or to phrase it in Scriptural terms, "[Y]ou shall know the truth, and the truth shall make you free" (John 8:32). But what is truth? From what does it liberate? And how does it accomplish this feat? By addressing these questions, we have attempted to reveal the close relationship between love and reality (what is true) and between sin and fantasy (what is false). Sin and its ill effects are nearly always rooted in self-deceit, whereas love and its benefits are byproducts of honesty and increasing awareness.

This book is founded on the conviction that the Bible is the supreme source of truth available to human beings regarding their spiritual nature, relationships and the world around them. A scientist may empirically discover functional truths that benefit mankind. For instance, he may come up with a cure for a dreaded disease or invent new materials that make technological advancements possible. Extending physical life and making earthly existence more comfortable are worthwhile ends, but they can hardly compare with providing a supreme purpose for living or securing one's eternal destiny.

The Bible, although scientifically reliable, is intended to secure larger goals than those of secular research. Scripture, although certainly pragmatically useful, is even more than that. It is intended as a source of absolute rather than relative truth. It reveals how life was intended to be lived and the way sin infringes on that goal. To understand human behavior one must understand sin. To understand sin, one must have unwavering confidence in Scripture: in its truthfulness and transcending power. Only then is man capable of genuine love. My prayer is that you will be unrelenting in your study of the Bible so that God may richly bless you in the neverending quest to love more and sin less.

# Answer Key

## Chapter 1

1. relationship; 2. the centrality of love; 3. association with others; 4. sin; 5. salvation; 6. 100 percent; 7. they are Jesus' disciples; 8. builds up (edifies); 9. war; 10. love

## Chapter 2

1. Satan; 2. Adam and Eve; 3. missing the mark, transgressing and lawlessness; 4. love; 5. relationships; 6. someone; 7. God; 8. the mind and or conscience; 9. psychological; 10. Scripture

## Chapter 3

1. natural revelation; 2. special revelation; 3. the incarnation; 4. spirit and life; 5. belief; 6. hearing the Word of God; 7. reality; 8. eyesight; 9. fantasy and illusion; 10. faith

## Chapter 4

1. unholy preoccupation with self; 2. one's own understanding; 3. life and immortality; 4. a military fortress or stronghold; 5. armor; 6. rain; 7. it guides; 8. it protects; 9. it nourishes; 10. Jesus loves me

# Chapter 5

1. dead; 2. corpse; 3. love and good works; 4. the Holy One of God; 5. love Jesus; 6. faith; 7. repentance; 8. baptism; 9. relationships; 10. Legion

# Chapter 6

1. deliverance (rescue) from sin and its consequences; 2. to love better; 3. reconciliation; 4. adoption; 5. redemption; 6. propitiation; 7. regeneration; 8. they are all relational; 9. selfishness; 10. love; 11. Adam

# Chapter 7

1. position, process, product; 2. to set apart or separate; 3. love; 4. a command to be obeyed; 5. God's Word; 6. a more thoughtful life; 7. God's Word and man's need; 8. balance; 9. growth-oriented; 10. judgment

# Chapter 8

1. A father's instruction; 2. a friend; 3. an enemy; 4. various trials; 5. temptation; 6. a way of escape; 7. the will; 8. forgiveness; 9. memory, imagination and volition; 10. what do you love?

# Chapter 9

1. the cross and the Word; 2. light; 3. love; 4. maturity, study, community and ministry; 5. doing good; 6. partaking of the Lord's Supper; 7. contentions; 8. souls; 9. sustain effort; 10. grace

# Chapter 10

1. Restore such a one; 2. gentleness; 3. you who are spiritual; 4. his own load; 5. his own work; 6. trespass; 7. they were brethren; 8. the law of Christ; 9. lest you also be tempted; 10. himself alone, and not in another

# Chapter 11

1. love; 2. joy; 3. peace; 4. longsuffering; 5. kindness; 6. goodness; 7. faithfulness; 8. gentleness; 9. self-control; 10. spiritual progression

## Chapter 12

1. change; 2. the knowledge of Christ; 3. love; 4. Expectancy Theory; 5. hope; 6. growth; 7. wastefulness; 8. heaven, health and harmony; 9. spiritual and physical health; 10. nagging, berating and threatening

## Chapter 13

1. threeness; 2. songwriting, painting and a sporting event; 3. echad; 4. Elohim; 5. one flesh; 6. Paul; 7. James; 8. the body of Christ; 9. the temple of God; 10. compassion, commission and cooperation